CW00733525

Social Media Income

How Solo Entrepreneurs and Small Companies can Make Money on Instagram and Other Social Media Platforms (2-in-1 collection)

Book 1: *Instagram Income: How Solo Entrepreneurs and Small Companies Can Make Money on IG*

Book 2: *Likes Don't Pay: Bills How to Leverage Social Media to Get Leads and Customers*

Chris Oberg

Contents

Book 1: Instagram Income: How Solo Entrepreneurs and Small Companies Can Make Money on IG

Introduction

We solo entrepreneurs and small business owners usually have one thing in common. We are always looking for ways to make more money, and the faster, the better! Therefore, our eyes are always open to new tactics and strategies for finding new leads and customers. As it happens, many of us turn to social media, particularly Instagram (IG), to market ourselves and our businesses.

As valuable as IG has the potential of being, IG is a tricky monster. If we are not careful, it eats up all our time and energy and spits us out with anxiety, brain fog, and a weird feeling of "gaaah...what am I doing wrong on IG?!"

I know, I've been there.

For me, IG was a frustrating time sink until a few months ago. When I first started marketing my business on IG, I did what most solo entrepreneurs do. I spent a ton of time on the platform, commenting on other posts, chasing more followers (because more is better right?), and" creating content." But, even if the numbers of followers slowly grew and my followers slowly started to engage more and more, something was missing. The missing part is obvious now, but I couldn't see it back then. The missing piece was that I didn't have a clear picture of where in my business my IG account lived, so I didn't have a clear strategy of how to monetize my IG account.

It took me a year and a half into my IG journey before I realized I had to view my IG account as an **INCOME STREAM** and not a "marketing channel." That slight mindset shift made a huge difference in my IG strategy. If you are serious about making money on IG, I highly suggest you start viewing IG as a potential income stream.

Why Should You Listen to Me when it comes to making money on IG?

I'm going to be very honest with you. I'm a regular Swedish guy living in Sweden. Swedish is my native language (I'm doing my best to hide my broken English). I coach solo entrepreneurs on building profitable self-publishing businesses on Amazon. I have had my IG account a while (check out my profile @inkomstmedbocker), and I have 900+ followers when I write this. 900 is not many followers, I'm aware of that, but you know what? You don't need a ton of followers to make money on IG, and I'm proof of that. Since I started to view my IG account as an <u>income stream</u> instead of a marketing channel a few months ago, I've since earned thousands of dollars and got hundreds of email subscribers from IG, proving you don't need a huge following to make money on IG.

I have no formal business background, but I've taken several great online business programs and courses (shout out to Ramit Sethi). Before starting my business journey, I dedicated a ton of time to online poker. Poker and business/entrepreneurship have a lot in common. Becoming successful in poker is all about seeing the world from other people's perspectives and making calculated strategic decisions based on the available information at hand. Combine that with the core of entrepreneurship (solving problems for a profit), and you have my background. In poker, like in business, good intentions are always lovely. But what matters is getting results. For me, results mean **making money**, which is what this book is all about.

3

What You'll Learn in This Book

Through these pages, I'm going show you strategies for using Instagram to get real paying customers. Then, we'll take a deep look into seeing how you can use IG to attract the right followers and turn them into paying customers.

In the opening chapter, we'll discuss Instagram's business model and how you can leverage it to your advantage. Then, we'll dive into some strategies for figuring out the purpose of your IG account and how you find a way to monetize your IG account. I'll also show you how to craft your strategy so that Instagram benefits from what you are doing.

The second chapter is all about figuring out your followers' heroes' journeys and finding a solution to their problems in a unique, engaging way. People are bombarded with thousands of images every day, so you must learn to connect with your followers.

The third chapter examines how everything you do on IG can be viewed as a product. We will also kill the expression "content creating" and start running your first money-making experiments. I'll show you some of my successful (and not so successful) IG experiments.

The fourth chapter is all about money and how to monetize your account, including different ways of selling products, different IG sales funnels, selling in DM, and much more.

Let's get started!

Chapter one: Figure out how you are going to make money on IG

I firmly believe that your money-making IG strategy should be aligned with IG's business model. If IG themselves likes what you are doing, your account will get more organic exposure, and IG will automatically push your IG account to more people. Here's how to accomplish that.

Instagram's Business Model

Why are people scrolling on IG? Simply put, they WANT to be distracted. They're looking for something that hooks their attention. The people scrolling on IG are the product of which IG is making money. IG is designed to make people spend as much time as possible on there. And for you to make money on IG, you need to create something that hooks the IG users' attention and makes them want to spend more time on IG. Therefore, your posts, videos, and all your content must be aligned with IG's business model.

Like most social media platforms, IG monetizes its platform by keeping people on there for as long as possible. Every little thing on IG, from the colors to the beeping sounds, is designed to trick people into spending more time on there. It's scary when you think about it, but that's the reality. For example, it's no coincidence that the IG feed is somewhat randomized, similar to a slot machine. You never know when you log in on IG. Will you hit the jackpot and find something that hooks your attention or not? Your IG feed is entirely different from mine because IG keeps serving content that interests and engages you, and it keeps serving me content that interests me. That way, we all end up happy.

While IG looks innocent from the outside with its clean interface and beautiful images, in reality, everything is carefully engineered with one goal in mind: monetize our attention. I like to use the analogy that IG is like a slot machine. In the same way, a slot machine keeps gamblers engaged and entertained, IG keeps us all entertained and distracted to make sure we spend as much of our free time on there as possible. And when you do, you are making money for IG. Once that happens, IG will throw you other stuff to grab your attention so that they can make even more money off you.

Knowing how IG is making money can help in many ways when you start crafting your money-making IG strategy. First, given how IG works, if your strategy aligns with IG's business model, you will increase the chances of IG picking up your account and recommending it to more people. Secondly, knowing that IG is like a slot machine that tries to monetize your attention can help to put clear boundaries around how you use IG. For example, the purpose of having an IG account is not to casually spend your valuable time and energy on IG. Instead, the goal is to use IG to make money for you and your business and do so while IG leaves a minimal footprint on your time and mental energy.

Your Business Model

Take a step back and look at your business from above. Look at all the ways people come to know about you, how they find your homepage, how they see your physical store if you have one, and how customers and clients refer you to their friends and family. Think about all the different paths these people take, from not knowing about you to doing business with you. Do you see all the different ways? Good. Now, think about where IG has a clear place in that mix.

In the early stages of my 1:1 coaching business, I didn't think too much about IG, focusing my attention and efforts on Facebook group posting and Google SEO (search engine optimization) instead. As a result, I thought that it was hard to sell on IG. The mistake I made was a classic one. I treated IG the same way I treated Google SEO. SEO lives at the top of the business funnel for most businesses, bringing in users looking for answers to questions or simple information about something.

On the other hand, IG is different and lives further down in the business funnel. Making money on IG comes down to grabbing attention and building engagement with one's followers. And when I talk about engagement, I don't mean a "like" on a post. Engagement for me means either commenting on or sharing my post, sending me a DM, or visiting my website.

When I shifted towards focusing on getting attention and engagement instead of "providing information," I quickly started to see the potential of IG. IG then helped me accomplish two things in my 1:1 coaching business. First, and most importantly, I was able to skyrocket the number of sales calls I booked from doing an attention/engagement stories-post --> DM conversation --> sales call. And secondly, I've got hundreds of email subscribers by pointing the URL in my profile to my lead magnet. For me, pretty much everything I do on IG either points people to contact me in DM or visit my website (with the end goal of them subscribing to my mailing list). That's how I monetize my IG account.

You might have a completely different business model. You might be able to monetize your IG account differently but to get you thinking about what you can do on IG, think about how your business is making money and where in your business IG fits the best. What type of products and services are you selling? Your IG strategy will be different if you run a 1:1 online coaching business as I do or if you own a local bakery and are trying to get more people to buy your cakes.

Having a clear goal for what you want to accomplish (more traffic to your e-commerce store? more email subscribers or sign-ups to your webinar, or booking more sales calls in IG DMs as I do?) will help you tremendously when you craft your money-making IG strategy. But before we talk more about strategy, let's figure out how to get the attention and engagement you first and foremost need to make money on IG.

How to get attention and engagement on IG

If we know that IG monetizes people's attention, we also know that you effectively have to get your followers' attention and engagement to make money on IG. If your followers scroll past your posts without any engagement, you will have difficulty making money on IG. So step one in your strategy should get your followers' attention.

If you haven't started your IG account yet, and don't have any followers yet, keep these tips in mind when you do.

One of the main reasons why people use IG daily is curiosity. When we find something that gets us curious and hooks our attention, our brain releases dopamine and serotonin, the "happy hormones," which give us a pleasant feeling. We crave that feeling! The IG slot machine does a fantastic job of delivering a boost of serotonin and dopamine. I'm not a neuroscience expert, but I know a few strategies for getting the right kind of attention and engagement on IG.

Connect, don't convince

It goes without saying, but whenever someone interacts with your IG account, they wish to receive value. Of course, the idea of value varies from one person to another. Still, you can think about your followers, prospects, and previous customers' hopes, fears, and dreams. That's what you want to connect to. What problem are you solving for your followers? What are the benefits they looking for? By connecting with their hopes, fears, and dreams, you are signaling that you understand them, care about them, and they will be more open to listening to what you have to say. In other words, you got their attention! Bingo!

Focusing on connecting instead of convincing stands out as authentic among all internet marketers out there. Think about it: if all you do on IG is try to convince your followers to buy your products, your followers will grow tired of you pretty damn fast. So instead, try one of these tips to connect with your followers.

Make It About Them and meet them where they are

Rather than rambling on about your product, try shifting things towards the issues of your followers. What would their needs be at this moment that caused them to seek out your IG account? What is something that is most important to them right now? Don't make it about you or your product; instead, make it about them. Ask them many questions and listen to what they have to say. You can DM them or do Q&As in stories and listen carefully to what they have to say. If you do that, you will have a well of valuable insight into why your followers are following you, and you can more easily connect with their hope, fears, and dreams.

I'm ALWAYS on the hunt for insight about my followers. In my coaching business, I coach people on making money by self-publishing on Amazon, but the REAL reason people are following me on IG has nothing to do with Amazon. They follow me because they want to learn how to gain more financial freedom in their lives, and that's the story I try to connect to. I could post self-publishing strategies all day long, but that would fall on deaf ears. So instead, I meet them where they are, and I can speak directly to their hope, fears, and dreams.

Asking for insight and what's going on inside your followers' minds opens up all kinds of opportunities. For example, you may have a testimonial from a previous client or a relevant case study. Since you know these people had similar concerns, you can connect more deeply with them.

Show Them You Care about them

If you wish to inspire your followers to do business with you, you need to put less of an emphasis on what you are selling and instead talk about the benefits of using your product or service. How will your product or service help them? Can you prove that you have already helped people like them before? Do you understand all of the problems that they are going through? Rather than talking about all your product's features, talk about its benefits and what it can do for them. Show that what you care about is solving their problem.

One of my entrepreneurial friends, Marie is doing this better than anyone I know. She has so much insight about her followers (mostly 25-55-year-old women looking to find their life's task). She can pretty much read her follower's minds, and the engagement she gets on her posts is insane! She speaks right to her followers' hearts and connects deeply. For example, when she launched her group coaching program, she made $8,000 from 600 followers in TWO DAYS! How cool isn't that? I'll share how she did it later in this book.

The purpose of your IG account

Start with your business model in mind, and think about what you want to accomplish with your IG account. Then work backward. If your goal is to bring more customers to your e-commerce store, your reason for having an IG account is to drive traffic, and everything you will do on IG must somehow support that goal. I'll show you a detailed example of how I use IG to drive traffic later in this book. On the other hand, if you are a physical therapist and are using IG to get new leads, your best strategy might be to personally contact all your existing and new followers, one by one, to build a relationship and connect with them.

Regardless of what you want to accomplish, think about how IG can benefit from what you are doing. Nobody knows how the IG algorithm works. You don't have to worry about that either as long as you focus on connecting with your followers, getting attention and engagement, and knowing how everything you post on IG fits within your business model.

Chapter two: Be the Guide on your followers heroes journey

One of the people I follow in the personal brand space is Mike Kim. Mike has a podcast, and he recently launched his instant bestselling book *You Are The Brand*. In episode #301 of Mike's podcast, he brought up an interesting idea that had been on my mind for years: that most of the so-called "influencers" basically have very little or sometimes *nothing* valuable to say. I usually call this the "influencer trap". Many people aspire to be "influencers," but they come at it from I-I-I point of view and think that simply sharing whatever message *they* feel like (like what they had for lunch) will gain them popularity and make them rich and famous. I think that's a big mistake many people make when they set out to make money on IG. I like Mikes's take on this because he divided "influence" into three categories. These three categories are experts, influencers, and thought leaders.

Experts have tons of knowledge and cutting-edge expertise, but almost nobody knows about them, and very few people follow them. Think about a math professor, for example.
Influencers, on the other hand (often), have little or no expert knowledge about a particular subject, but many people (somehow) follow them.

The combination of both of them, with expert knowledge and many followers, is what Mike calls "thought leaders." Think about someone like Tony Robins in the personal development space.

If we take Mike's concept of "thought leaders," and instead of just applying it to personal brand business, we apply it to small companies as well, what we end up with is something we can call a "Guide."

Be the Guide

If there's something we humans love, it's a good old hero's journey, especially if we are the hero. With that journey in mind, you know the story where the hero overcomes all kinds of obstacles only to crash again, feel overwhelmed, dust their shoulders off, and keep going to reach his or her full potential. That's how you need to view your IG followers. They are heroes on their journey. So, what does that make you? You are the Guide, or rather, your company sells the guiding principles, the solution, the equipment, and the training. Your company is the compass the heroes will follow. They'll look to you for inspiration, motivation, and the resources to keep going even on the darkest of nights. They'll look to your IG posts for the voice of reassurance.

Generally speaking, people's main life challenges are lack of money, health, or unsuccessful relationships. People are likely following you to solve a problem in one of these areas. Your business can be a guide to those looking for financial freedom, success, or better health. You can provide them with the tools they need to get there and show them how to use these tools effectively by being their Guide on IG.

14

Once you gather a following that begins to trust you and see you as the Guide, that's when your IG income potential will start to blossom. It is tough to monetize IG, even if you have plenty of followers, if you don't solve real problems for real people. Positioning yourself as the Guide and having real influence gives you much more leverage to sell your products on IG, and the beautiful benefit of this approach is that you don't need tons of followers to make money on IG. In my opinion, this approach allows you to monetize your IG account from day one.

Being the Guide and having real influence is understanding the challenges your followers' experience, then providing a solution uniquely and interestingly. By doing so, your IG account will become like a magnet that draws people in, and you can do this in all niches.

Becoming the Guide is a relatively easy, but not a simple, endeavor. The hard part is finding what your market wants to read, seeing what they're interested in, and creating solutions to their problems.

Compare the Guide approach to the standard influencer approach. Guides don't call themselves "influencers." They don't feel the need to label themselves as influencers. They're too busy doing exciting stuff and sharing their ideas with their followers. However, many tend to label themselves as "influencers" without having any real influence. These people are called influencers, not because of their advice or the content they produce but because they have many followers. Self-proclaimed influencers are full of themselves, share shallow ideas, and force useless content down our throats, and by the way, most of them are struggling to make money on IG.

To become the Guide, you need to be an interesting individual with interesting things to share, and you need to be authentic in your way. Naturally, that is easier said than done, but it offers an alternative to the term "influencer" many of us are getting tired of.

In today's marketing world, there's much talk about "content creation." But is that the only thing that matters to make money on IG? I don't think so. What is often missing is being interesting and connecting to your followers. Many so-called "content creators" settle for putting out tons of shallow content, which builds a nice library of content, sure, but that's not what IG is about. A library of the content does not equal money in the bank.

Being interesting, authentic, and focusing on your money-making IG strategy (getting attention, engagement, and leading people where you want them to go), that's what is going to earn you money.

As previously touched upon, when you approach IG with a connecting mentality, you need to ask your followers the right questions to get the proper insight. And with the right insight, you use these as building blocks for all your content. That way, you can soon read your followers' minds like my friend Marie.

Each of your followers has different hopes, fears, and dreams and has their hero's journey. To connect with them, you must ask them questions, even if it is scary at first. You can ask them questions in many ways; preferably, I try to get my followers on a video call, but DM works fine too.

Figure out your followers' real pain points

I've borrowed this three-step structure from Ramit Sethi. Every time I get the chance to chat with one of my followers and feel like they can open up, I rely on this structure in my hunt for insights.

1. Get them to open Up

When you ask a question to a follower, you need to do it in a manner that will get them to open up to you. For example, let's say that your question has many facts wrapped into it. As a result, instead of being a question like it is supposed to be, it ends up being a statement where you are looking for agreement or feedback. But unfortunately, this doesn't pave the way for the follower to open up to you.

To get your follower to open up, you might want to ask them short questions asked in a simple form. Focus on whys and hows and give them incentives to open up to you. "Can you explain that, please," or "could you offer some examples" are a great way to get things started.

Connecting with your followers is a two-way street. Not only do you need to connect with them, but they need to connect with you as well. This is the only way that they will be able to open up to you.

2. Discover Their Needs

Every question that you ask must have a purpose – and in this case, it should be to find out their needs. If you managed to get the follower to open up in the first stage, you need to get them to spill out the right info. Many questions may help you out for that purpose, but here are just some of them that you can use:

- What made you interested in following this account? [they might answer something like, "I want to learn more about how to get in shape"]
- What is the main thing that is preventing you from achieving [insert the outcome they want]
- What are your short-term goals? What about the long-term ones?
- Are there any ways for me/us to better meet your needs?
- What do you consider to be your priorities right now?

The questions may change depending on your niche, the service you are providing, and the follower you are dealing with. Sometimes, the best way could be to jump the gun right away with the question, "what are your current needs?" and when they answer, say, "Great, I have a product that will help you accomplish that. Would you be willing to book a 30-min sales call to see if it's a good fit?"

Also, you must be aware that you'll have to ask many follow-up questions. Sometimes, even the customer may not know what their need is – so, you'll have to tap into their mind to find out.

3. Be Careful with Emotional Landmines

How often have you asked a question to a prospect, client, or follower only to see everything eventually blow up in your direction? I remember one particular time when that happened to me. This one lady reached out to me, asked a few questions, and asked if we could book a 30-min consultation call. My first thought was, "yes! She wants to buy my program! I better get on that call!". We booked the call three days later, but that didn't stop her from emailing me long emails days before the call. Those were very emotional emails, including her desires, her broken dreams, and how society didn't believe in her.

We got on the call three days later. My initial plan was obviously to sell my coaching program, but that call somehow turned into a 1,5hr therapy session. When I asked her why she reached out to me, she told me her entire back story. And when we talked about price, it became obvious to me that she had no buying intent whatsoever. I was completely drained after that call, but the lesson was a good one: if you sense that you have stepped on the wrong emotional landmine, get the hell out of there asap!

However, if you step on the right emotional landmine, you might trigger an even stronger connection with your follower by using their emotions to your advantage.

Think about the many times you blurted out your needs just because you got emotional about something. It's in our nature – and you can be sure this will happen to your followers as well. This is why it's wise to ask questions that evoke emotions – for example, desire, arousal, and so on.

Strategies for creating connecting content

Everything suddenly becomes interesting when you set out to help your followers on their journey by showcasing empathy and staying true to yourself. Everything they say to you can be used to create posts that connect with them. With the two simple questions, "Which hero's journey am I helping with?" and "How am I helping?" you can find ideas everywhere.

I like to read, and books contain valuable ideas. When I read, I always look for small concepts, quotes, or something that feels authentic and how that can relate to my followers. That said, you can also draw ideas from movies, TV shows, artwork, or anywhere else. If you can figure out how to connect your content to these bigger sources, you can easily inspire people and guide them on their own hero's journey.

Developing a form of unique taste

What distinguishes the "shallow" content from the transformative and follow-worthy content you're going to post is your taste and how you blend your ideas with taste. Developing a form of unique taste and how you solve your followers' hero's journey is what will help to make you interesting. Invariably, that taste can only come from developing a solid ground and knowledge about your followers and everything related to them. Perhaps you have a taste for history, so you include in a lot of historical anecdotes, or you have a taste for a particular cuisine, so you blend your content with that, or you have a strong taste for a certain type of fashion, and you develop something around that.

This is why the two-pronged approach of understanding your audience (what's important to them, what hero's journey they're on, what problems you solve for them) and developing your taste is so important. It helps you connect with your audience in a way they'll find interesting and also helps you find ideas about what could be interesting to them.

Sharing what you know also means sharing your mistakes or failures so that others can learn from them and save themselves the time, effort, and financial resources you've invested in learning those lessons. You can share both your own and others' personal stories, provide tips on how to solve problems, solutions to problems you've solved for your audience in the past, and more. The most important thing about sharing what you know is that, by doing so, you develop your taste when it comes to the things that interest your followers. Think of it as your emotional fingerprint. The only way to develop your emotional fingerprint is by keeping an eye on what interests your followers and staying in touch with them.

Lastly, but importantly, because Instagram is a platform where people discover new content, you can afford to experiment with different types of content. For instance, you can upload photos of the things you love, links to articles or interviews with influencers in your industry, fun facts about your line of work, and anything related to your niche or interests. Bottom line, it doesn't matter what type of content you upload as long as it's interesting and relevant to your target audience.

Exercise: brainstorm ten different posts

It's time to package everything we have covered so far and start experimenting on IG. The only way to make money on IG is to get practical, which means posting, testing, and seeking honest feedback from your followers. Think about how you can position yourself as the hero on your followers' journey and brainstorm a few different ideas you can turn into IG posts.

Chapter three: Running Your Money Making Experiments

IG **offers the** perfect environment for running money-making experiments. You can make a post in under 30 minutes and almost instantly see if you hit your target or not. If a particular type of post catches your followers' attention and yields the results you're after, do more of that! And if a specific kind of post flops, great! You view that as a valuable experiment and try the next thing. Your strategy should be a bit loose and fluid, constantly experimenting with new things to crack the winning formula of what resonates with your followers. In this chapter, I will show you how to run these experiments at rapid speed, viewing everything you post on IG as a *product*.

If you are new to IG with zero followers

If you are just getting started on IG and have zero or very few followers, you are in for a treat! It seems like the IG algorithm is pushing and boosting new accounts to (much) more organic exposure compared to older accounts. It makes sense that IG does that. IG wants you (the user) to get as many followers as fast as possible because then you will feel like many people are hyped about what you are doing, which will make you spend more time on IG (so IG can monetize your attention). More than that, IG wants to keep recommending new accounts in their "discovery feed" for users to explore.

When you are new to IG, I just want you to be careful. The purpose of having an IG account is to make money and contribute to your business's bottom line. It's not about chasing random followers or getting hyped about how many "likes" you get.

If you have an existing following on IG

Regardless of whether you have a small or large IG following, and regardless of your previous IG strategies, be ready to lose some of your followers as soon as you start these money-making experiments. Losing followers hurts, but it's a good thing. Followers who are not interested in what you offer are dead weight, and you want to segment your existing followers as soon as possible to remove that weight. That being said, you will eventually get more new followers, but older accounts are a bit tricky to "wake up" and require more work before the algorithm picks them up and starts "boosting" them like new accounts. Therefore, you might lose more followers than you gain when beginning with this new approach.

See All Your IG Posts as Products

Eli Schwart's book Product Led SEO truly opened my eyes to SEO. In that book, Eli talks about why most SEO strategies are flawed (they tend to only focus on Google rankings) and why every SEO effort should be viewed as being a *product*. He means that every piece of SEO content should be carefully designed to attract the customers' desires and lead them somewhere with the end goal of turning them into customers. I love that concept. Just think about it… How many times haven't you heard that SEO is all about rankings? Sure, rankings may be important but ranking high on Google isn't worth anything unless the traffic contributes to the bottom line.

When I read Eli's book, I got an epiphany moment when I understood that the same concept could be applied to IG! I blew my mind when I realized that everything I do on IG could be viewed as a PRODUCT. Everything you post on IG, whether they're feed-posts, stories, or videos, have a few ingredients. You have an image or video file, written text, and most important of all, the underlying "problem" (or hero's journey) your content (post, story, video) is supporting. When you package all those ingredients, you have a product. A feed-post is a type of product. A stories-post is a product. A 20-sec reel is a product. Everything your followers consume from you can be viewed as a product.

When your followers are using your product (namely, consuming your content), the product guides your followers throughout their journey so that they'll want to use more of your products. Posting on IG then becomes a kind of chain where every post is a small product.

The purpose of a product is to make money

The purpose of putting out a product (posting on IG) should be to make money. However, it doesn't mean all your posts have to be sales posts, but rather that all your posts should fit within your business funnel. Now, here's the big difference between this approach and the "content creation" approach. When a "content creator" posts something, more often than not, it does not sync with the overall business funnel and therefore does not contribute to the business bottom line.

Two of my money-making experiments

When you start thinking about which product to create, spend a few minutes planning out what you want to accomplish with the product you have in mind. If you are doing a feed-post, what are you hoping to accomplish? When I do a feed-post, I want people to comment, and I want to take the conversation to DM and work my magic there. Here's an example of how I did that with a simple feed video experiment.

Look at this video here:

The quality is pretty bad, the lighting is bad, and I'm looking a bit tired too. And it only got 225 views and five comments. What a failure! Or?

No.

What's not showing here is how this video made me $400.

Take a look at those comments below the video.

That's real engagement. She is interested in what I'm saying. When you get real engagement in comments like this, consider that green light to move the conversation to DM.

We chatted in DM, and I did my best to connect with her in my hunt for more insights into her desires.

From DM, we took the conversation to email and onto Zoom, and she signed up for one of my coaching programs.

That's a long funnel, I know. It's many steps from the comments to the sale, but that's what a simple video experiment can result in, even if I look like a "failure" from the outside.

Lesson learned from this test:
Don't overthink your experiments. Even an "ugly" video with 225 views can make money on IG... as long as it fits within your business funnel!

I love selling in IG stories. For me, stories are the most powerful sales tool on IG. IG recently added the ability for all of us to include URL links in our stories, which is super powerful. My default strategy for selling in IG stories is to have 3-5 slides, divided into three categories. The first category is aimed at getting attention and connection, the second is to build some context, and the third is to direct/link my followers to a website or encourage them to take some kind of action.

Here's a story-funnel I spent 2 hours doing and got zero engagement (this story was originally posted in Swedish):

ARE YOU HAPPY WITH HOW MUCH MONEY YOU ARE MAKING?	MOST PEOPLE ARE NOT. THEY WANT TO MAKE MORE A LOT MORE.	THEY WANT TO EARN PASSIVE INCOME
1	2	3
ONE WAY TO EARN PASSIVE INCOME IS TO PUBLISH BOOKS ON AMAZON.	AMAZON CAN SELL YOUR BOOKS FOR YOU.	MY BOOKS HAVE MADE OVER $12,000 IN PASSIVE INCOME THIS YEAR.
4	5	6
YOU CAN START YOUR OWN PUBLISHING BUSINESS IN ALMOST NO TIME	ARE YOU READY TO MAKE PASSIVE INCOME ON AMAZON? REACH OUT TO ME IN DM, AND LET'S TALK!	
7	8	

Can you see why this test didn't work?

Looking at this eight-slide funnel now, It's clear to me that this funnel is way too long and probably a bit too boring as well. I should have shortened it, changed the fonts and images, and talked about the benefits of my coaching programs much more. But hey, I didn't, and that's fine. I simply wrote that off as a valuable experiment and kept my head high.

Are you ready to start experimenting with your products?

Create Your Product

It's time to package everything we have talked about so far and create your product (aka, doing your posts). Take everything into account and think about how you are the guide, think about your followers' hero's journey, their underlying questions, include your unique taste, take the plunge, and create your product. Most IG pros advocate for "content categories" or "content buckets," which means a few broad categories you constantly produce products (create content) around. For a wellness coach, that might be one around exercising, one around dieting, and one around recovering and resting. You can go as broad or narrow as you wish. Typically, I don't overthink the content buckets that much, yet it's a strategy to keep in mind to make sure you connect with all types of people within your niche.

For instance, let's say you decide to run an experiment with a two-slide feed post. For doing that, you need an image, and you need to write some copy. So here's how to get it right:

Start your Canva account

Countless tools can help facilitate and perfect your IG game. For example, I create my posts in Canva. Canva is an online graphic design tool that makes photo editing a breeze. It has a massive database of free images, fonts, and layouts for you to use to create beautiful, eye-catching posts. Set up a Canva account (canva.com) and look around at their layouts.

29

Picking the right image

Instagram is a highly visible platform, meaning that the image is a big part of your product. The general rule is to design something that "breaks through the noise", while knowing that the goal of your product is to connect with your followers on their journey. In other words, you don't want to stand out for the wrong reasons but rather fit in within the context of the problem you're trying to solve. You are not concerned about standing out for the sake of standing out since that will never lead to more sales. Instead, you want your images to be like a magnet that your followers will enjoy.

I'm not a very talented visual artist, and my design skills are limited. My strategy has always been to let my copywriting skills do more of the selling. That said, if your image sucks, it's going to be hard to get the attention you need to make money. I recommend starting with something extremely basic, like a white background or a simple image. That's enough in the testing phase. The purpose is not to get it perfect; the purpose is to get started.

For the sake of this experiment, let's pretend you are an online yoga instructor, and your purpose for using IG is to get more leads and signups to your online course. You have tried IG before, but it didn't really "click, " and you are now giving it a new shoot. Your first step should be to choose an image that matches your followers' hero's journey. For example, their hero's journey could be "living a stress-free life," so you pick an image that's signals yoga and calmness, like this one:

Let's keep that image and move on to what you write in your image and your caption.

Copywriting for IG

Copywriting is the most undervalued skill in marketing. I don't know why, maybe because it's sexier to talk about ad spend and the hottest hashtags of the day? But let's be real here, getting good at copywriting can dramatically improve how much money you make on IG. Everything you write on IG is copywriting in one form or another—every single word. The text you include in your images is copywriting. The text you write in your caption is copywriting. Everything you write is copywriting.

The copywriting formula AIDA

There are many different formulas for writing copy, and there are many different forms of copy. I highly recommend you take the time to learn the different types of copy you write in your business. Still, as a starting point for writing good enough IG posts, I recommend AIDA's classic copywriting formula. AIDA stands for attention, interest, desire, and action.

Attention

Step number one is always to get people's attention. If you can't get their attention, it will be hard to accomplish anything. How do you get someone's attention on IG? It's not easy these days, but there are a few things you can do. First of all, you need to write directly to your target market. The words you use must be tailored to your target market. Making money on IG is not about getting everyone's attention and "breaking through the noise," as discussed earlier. It's getting the right people's attention. That's all that matters. When you design your images, don't think about what you think "looks good." Think instead about your target market. The same goes for headlines. Don't write "catchy" headlines for the sake of being catchy. Write headlines that resonate with your market!

Interest/Desire

When you have got your target market's attention, now what? Now it's time to start digging deeper, getting them to listen to what you have to say. This is the trickiest part. If you got their attention but didn't follow up with something interesting, they will most likely continue scrolling and never return.

Let's say you write an attention-grabbing image text and get your ideal customer to stop their scroll. What you need to do now is to build up interest by sharing something they care about. You can do that by telling a story that resonates with them or talking about anything related to their hopes, fears, and dreams. The trick here is always to think, "what's in it for them? What's in it for them?" It's not about you at this stage; it's about them. It's about their interest, not yours.

When you nail the interest/desire part of your copy, your audience wants MORE. The copy you wrote has aroused them, got their blood pumping, and the dopamine flowing in their bodies. They want more, and they want it NOW.

Do you see how that works? You are not forcing them on anything at this point; you have grabbed their attention and built up their interest. You are almost there; all you need now is not to screw up the action part.

Action

You have probably heard of the term CTA before, which stands for *call to action*. CTAs are super important in copywriting. CTAs are what make people buy your stuff, sign up for your email list, reach out to you, like your posts (not that important, but it's still an action), and tell their friends about how awesome you are.

A CTA is a prompt, statement, or question at the end of your copy that works like an invisible hand that gets people to act on whatever you want them to act upon.
Here's the one thing that most people miss with a good CTA: you can never force someone to do something. An act must come from within; otherwise, it's manipulation. If you have done your job by getting their attention and making them interested in what you have to say, the CTA doesn't need to be written in bold letters with tons of exclamation marks. All you need to do is lead them wherever you want them to go.

Many people talk about CTA as if it's all that matters, but they are wrong. A CTA itself can rarely do all the heavy lifting. As the business owner, you must get your prospects' attention, take them on a journey in your interest/desire phase, and leave them with the decision to act on your CTA. If you have done your job right, they will almost always act on the CTA. The key here (again) is to be authentic and know your audience, focusing on them and always asking yourself, "what's in it for them."

Copy in the image

For me, including some written text in my images works better than not doing it, but I've heard that many people report the opposite. Selfies are the best, they say. Test what works best for you, but if you decide to include some text in your images, here's how I would do it.

If you decide to do a one slide feed post

Consider the written text in your image as a "headline." Writing good headlines can be tricky and require some training. A few tips on writing a good headline:

- Include digits instead of words, like "5" instead of "five."
- Be extremely specific.
- Create urgency and frame it as a "secret" or an "idea"

If we go back to the yoga example above and want to make a product about the five benefits of yoga, we could write a headline that says "Five Benefits of doing Yoga." That's not bad, but it's not particularly good either. On the other hand, if we change that headline to "5 secret benefits of doing yoga," I'm sure more people would stop their scroll and read our post.

If you have two or more images

A popular trend is to include all text in the images and post several images in one post like a carousel. This works so well because it's much easier to read for the user than reading a long caption. Remember to follow the AIDA formula and learn from my eight-slide story-funnel above if you decide to do that. Another benefit of including more than one image in your post is that IG gives every post a second chance and will use the second image as the "front image" when they show the post the second time.

Writing captions

The caption is the text that's below the image. The first part of the caption, the text visible before the "read more" is your attention part. The "read more" button is there because IG knows that most people are not reading the caption.

I think the best type of captions is like an image extension, and it's clear that the image and the caption work together. I've played around with different types of caption openers and what works best for me speaks directly to my followers. I try to avoid "I," "my," and other self-centric openers when I write captions. To get the right tone and voice in my captions, I always do the images first and write caption afterward, and I look at the image when I write the caption. That way, the image and the caption have the same vibe.

Stories copy

Your followers have no idea what you have posted in stories before they open up your stories. Therefore, your stories' open rate is critical to get the most out of your stories. I recommend mixing things up in stories to make your followers curious about what you have posted. If you are doing 99% sales stories, your followers will quickly grow tired of you and stop opening your stories. I use stories to sell, drive traffic, build engagement, entertain, inform, and do all kinds of things! Since you can post several stories slides in a row, similar to a "sales funnel," you can take your followers on a little stories journey.

If you decide to try a stories funnel with the end goal of generating traffic back to your website, a thing I've noticed is including the CTA two times to increase the chance of your followers acting on it.

Look at this funnel:

Attention   Connection   CTA 1   CTA 2

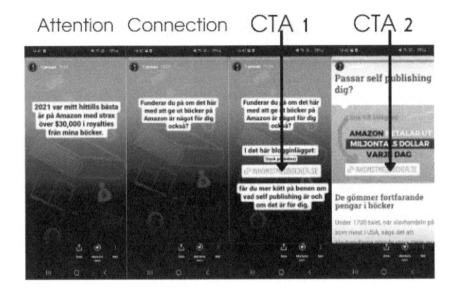

Result in traffic:

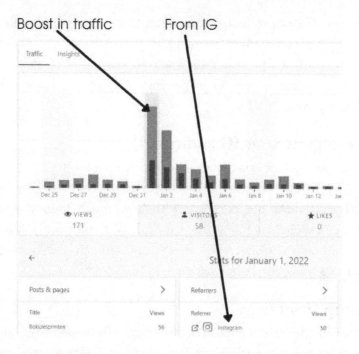

Keep the winners and seek actual proof

I would encourage you to start experimenting and putting your products out there as soon as possible. There is no better way to make money on IG than doing the work. That being said, The market will tell you if your post resonated or not. If you hear nothing, that's the market telling you loud and clear that your product (posts) wasn't a good fit. If that happens, try something new! On the other hand, if you get a ton of responses, likes, DMs, that's the market telling you your posts did resonate, and I would recommend you to do all you can to lead those people closer to a sale by setting up sales calls, sending links to your products or inviting them to your store. Spending time following up and speaking directly to your followers will multiply your chances of making money on IG.

When you find a product combination that's working, double down on that. And remember, working is more than just "likes." The ultimate proof of a product's success is if you get IG to make money, so if you manage to get IG to generate revenue, well done! You've cracked the code.

How to grow your IG audience

A common topic of conversation about making money on IG is how to grow your IG following best. However, as you know, the number of followers does not correlate with how much money a specific person is making on IG. With that said, you still need followers to make money on IG, and you need some strategy for keeping your account growing at a steady pace.

The top 50 strategy

In Russell Brunson's book *Traffic Secrets*, Brunson talks about a strategy he has successfully used to grow his podcast, email list, and social channels. He calls it the top 100 strategy. The basic idea of that strategy is to build relationships with the top 100 accounts within your niche. All the followers you want are probably already following one of the top 100 accounts within your niche. So when you build a relationship with the top 100 accounts, it becomes like a bridge between you and the followers you are after.

I think the top 100 strategy is a perfect example of an honest, authentic strategy to grow your account, but following 100 large IG accounts in your niche may seem a bit much, so I have moderated Russell's strategy to the top 50 strategy.

How the top 50 strategy works in practice:

Start following 50 large accounts in your niche and gradually build a relationship with those accounts by liking their photos, commenting on relevant posts, writing with them in DM, etc. For this strategy to work, you need to be genuinely interested in knowing them. You do not want them to get the feeling that you are writing to them just because you want something in return. As soon as you have a somewhat established relationship with one or more of the larger accounts, start sharing their posts in your stories. Then it is only a matter of time before they share one of your posts or stick one of your comments in their comment field. Once that happens, you will see a flood of new followers starting to follow you.

I've used the top 50 strategy to get more followers, and it works great. Sweden is a relatively small country, so my 900+ followers may not look so impressive, but it is easier said than done to grow an account to the magic 10k limit in Sweden.

Use IG's new features

One way to increase the spread of your posts and thus increase the chances of getting new followers is to use IG's latest features. As I write this, IG reels are the latest feature that seems to provide the best spread, but IG is constantly updating and changing the platform, so it may be that reels have been removed when you are reading this. So, ask yourself which is the newest feature on IG right now and use it as much as you possibly can.

Algorithm pushes

We all love tactics and strategies for getting more followers, but the best (and most difficult) way to grow on IG is to get IG to pick up your account and start recommending it on its own. If you scroll in your feed, you will see a section called "suggestions for you." If you click around in stories, you will see the same section there. These are areas that IG itself uses to promote accounts. IG could very well have used this space for ads instead, but they want you as a user to find new accounts to follow so that you get the best experience out of using IG. In addition, IG keeps a close eye on what preferences we have, what pictures we like, and what posts we read. In this way, IG can tailor individual account recommendations to all of us.

For IG to pick up your account, IG needs to know what type of account you have. Otherwise, they can never recommend your account to the right user. I who follow many business accounts usually get suggestions to follow other business accounts. I never get suggestions on following home decorating accounts or cooking accounts. IG knows what kind of posts I like and does its best to make it easy for me to find more similar accounts, so that I spend more time on the platform. Take an extra look at the type of accounts you get as" suggestions for you," which indicates what IG thinks your account is about.

Some common pitfalls make it difficult for IG to know what type of account you have. In the short term, these pitfalls can get you new followers, but it destroys your chances of growing in the long run. The most common of these pitfalls is to jump on the so-called "follower train," which means about 20 accounts begin to follow each other. The problem with this is that as long as not all of these 20 accounts are within the same niche, IG gets confused about your target audience, and IG has a hard time knowing whom to recommend your account to. If you have several followers who in turn follow accounts in training, horse jumping, home decor, but you have a business in cooking, then you have a problem.

Another common pitfall is "giveaways," which means that you give away a prize to everyone who likes one of your posts and chooses to follow you. Unfortunately, if you host giveaways, you will also confuse IG, as lots of people will start following you to be in the draw for a prize.

The timeless strategy for growing your IG account is to always provide awesome products (posts) to your target audience. It is the only thing that will work if you have IG as a source of income.

Hashtags

A user on IG can choose to follow specific hashtags. A hashtag looks like this "#" and is a type of "category" of posts. For example, if someone posts a post with #summer, it will be visible to some followers who have chosen to follow the hashtag #summer.

Sometimes there is much chatter around finding the "best" hashtags, but I think hashtags are a bit overrated. Once you have posted a post, you can look at the post's statistics. For example, you can see how many extra impressions the post got from your hashtags. Usually, it is about 5-10% extra impression from hashtags.

Hashtags give an extra small boost to the spread, which can get you more followers. Still, my recommendation is to make awesome posts and choose relevant hashtags without overthinking them.

Chapter four: Monetize Your IG account

The tricky part about selling on IG is the same as other online selling channels. Your followers must know you are selling something, which means you must talk about your products and services in your posts. Consistency is key here. Simply mentioning it here and there won't magically get your followers to hand you money. In this chapter, we will look at different ways to monetize your IG account.

Marketing rule of 7

There is a "marketing rule of 7" rule in sales and marketing. That rule says a person on average needs to be exposed to a product/service seven times before the person in question buys the product/service. These exposures can be called contact points. A contact point can be to see a product in the IG feed, IG stories, hear about it on a podcast, or have a friend recommend it. The rule of seven applies to the highest degree to everything you sell on IG.

To visualize how the rule of seven works, let's pretend you have 1 000 followers on IG, and all your followers see your offer seven times, making it a total of 7 000 impressions. Now, pretend instead that you have 7 000 followers, and everyone sees your offer one time, which is also 7 000 impressions.

In which scenario do you think you would have sold the most?

If the marketing rule of 7 is true, you would have sold more if the same 1,000 people had seen your offer seven times compared to if 7,000 different people had seen it only once. The reason why is quite simple. Humans are drawn to what we recognize and are often not as attracted to foreign things.

Putting the rule of seven in motion is about increasing the number of contact points between your followers and your offer. Of course, it's easier said than done, but the key here is to keep putting the same offer in front of the same people in different ways.

Talk about your offer in stories

Stories automatically disappear after 24 hours, so you want to make sure people see them. As I've said before, stories are my favorite sales tool on IG. You can use stories to generate leads, drive traffic, draw attention to certain products or even ask your followers specific questions. You can do so much in stories. Only your imagination will be the limit.

The IG stories sales funnel

A simple framework I've used in stories multiple times with great results is the mini sales funnel, typically 3-6 slides and built on top of the AIDA copywriting formula.

The goal of the first slide is to get my followers' attention, so they keep reading to the next slide. If you look at the left corner in your stories, you can see how many of your followers have seen that particular slide, which means that you can track how many people see slide 1, slide 2, slide 3, etc. Seeing how many people are opening your stories is important information because that can signal if they are interested in what you have to say. I usually have a story open rate of around 20%, and I'm happy with that. If you have a very low open rate, consider changing your profile picture.

The goal of slides 2-3 is to build desire and have my followers keep reading. I'm usually trying to connect to the benefits of using my product in these slides.

Slides 4-6 are all about getting my followers to act. Acting usually means sending a DM or visiting my website. Depending on what you sell, acting can mean a bunch of things. And as I said before, whenever you get a DM from someone, treat it seriously. The person is most likely interested in what you have to offer.

Talk about your offer in IG Live Video

This is a relatively new feature. It's a type of video streamed on the platform as it's being recorded, meaning you can broadcast your videos live to your followers. This is an excellent idea for businesses looking to build stronger relationships with their followers. The benefit of Instagram Live is it's more engaging than any other form of video. People can comment and ask questions in real-time, and you can answer and engage with them.

This way, you could easily make monthly updates by reading and replying to comments or by making videos in response to the comments. This is an excellent way to communicate with your target audience and allow them to connect with you on a more personal level. IG Live is also great for making announcements if you have important news to share with your followers. Here are some tips to help you make the most of IG Live:

- Be prepared to respond to real-time comments during your broadcast.
- Don't broadcast forever. Limit your broadcast to 30 minutes to keep people engaged and wanting more.
- Make sure you tell people that you'll be going live on Instagram in advance.

Going live is fairly simple, and it only takes a few clicks to start broadcasting. Once you start your broadcast, your followers will see your story in the "Live" top section of their feed. You can even set up multiple cameras to broadcast different angles. Let's take the example of the Instagrammer @adrian_rodriguez. He owns a fitness company that offers personalized plans to help people get into shape. Adrian regularly uses Instagram Live to broadcast his workouts in real-time, which his followers love!

Talk about your offer in your feed - the living room strategy

There's much talk about whether it's important to have an organized and nice-looking feed or not. In my opinion, as long as you haven't nailed everything else we have talked about in this book, a nice-looking feed is not magically going to get your followers to hand you money. In my experience, feed posts can contribute to sales, but stories are a much more effective sales tool. So is the feed not important? It is. When I think about the IG feed, I think about entering a living room. I have a little bit of everything in my living room; photos, arts, furniture, instruments, and books. In my opinion, the IG feed is kind of a living room. When new potential followers check out your feed, they usually skim the first 6-9 posts. If all you do is showcase your product and do promo, promo, and promo, what will they think? They might not want to follow you. On the other hand, if you have that living room vibe on your feed, it feels connected, and you are inviting them to follow you. I've had people coming to my feed and instantly reaching out for coaching because my feed connected with them.

Plan your feed posts in advance

An exercise I started with recently is to plan my feed posts in advance. The way I do it is simple and requires a simple pen and paper. I draw 12 squares, each representing a slot in my feed. I try to do two feed posts per week, which means I plan my feed six weeks in advance. What I try to accomplish with this planning exercise is a nice balance between all areas of my business and making sure I get that living room vibe in my feed.

Here's how the exercise looks:

IG plan

Benefits of self publishing	Engagement video	Pic of me outside
Date:	Date:	Date:
FAQ	Book recommendation: Profit First	Royalties feb
Date:	Date:	Date:
Video: Current trends on Amz	Testimonial from client	Pic when I sit in the couch and read
Date:	Date:	Date:
Start up costs	Three tips for making money on Amazon	Post about my lead magne
Date:	Date:	Date:

If you want to do this exercise yourself, think about how all these posts will fit in your overall business funnel. Remember, the goal is not just to post beautiful images. The goal is to connect with your followers on their heroes' journeys.

Ask for testimonials and feature People Who Use Your Product

One way to talk about your offer without talking about it is to use testimonials from previous customers. When I ask about testimonials, I send my customers six questions. Here are the six questions I use when I ask for testimonials about my coaching program.

1. What was your biggest concern before buying my coaching program?

2. What kind of result have you got from taking the program?

3. Can you mention one thing that was over your expectations?

4. Can you mention two more things you were happy with?

5. Would you recommend other people to buy this program? If so, why?

6. Is there something you want to change/add to the program?

Depending on what you sell, one way of keeping your product relevant to your audience and keeping the marking rule of seven going is by giving your followers insights into the type of people who are using your product. This is a popular strategy within the wellness industry. For example, paying for big-name influencers to wear a piece of clothing. Personally, I would not overspend on this strategy at the beginning. As long as you have a deep interest in giving your followers what they want and connecting with them, you don't need to hire expensive influencers to market your products.

Think in terms of campaigns, not posts

When you know the purpose of your IG account and where in your business IG lives, it becomes clear that IG is just a tool to grow your business. To make money and grow your business, you need to sell something, and to sell something, your best bet is to run som kind of campaign. There are tons of different kinds of campaigns, including launch campaigns, traffic campaigns, awareness campaigns, etc.

When I talk about campaigns here, I don't mean paid ads. What I mean by a campaign is the collection of all your efforts during a limited time to reach a specific goal. It's all the posts, videos, reels, and stories you are doing during a fixed period (3 days, seven days, or 30 days) to get your followers to buy whatever you are selling.

Plan to the end

You can keep a few things in mind to increase the chances of running a successful campaign. The first thing is to plan to the end, which means mapping out all the posts, videos, reels, etc. you will do before you start. Then, all you need to do is execute your plan, which is much easier than winging it and posting whatever you feel like. The second thing to keep in mind to run a successful campaign is to set a goal of what you hope to accomplish. By planning and setting goals, you have something to measure and evaluate afterward, and it's easier to draw valuable lessons from your efforts.

Your campaign window

The most common campaign strategy is to focus all your efforts during a limited period. Of course, you have to decide which period works for you, but I recommend trying at least three to seven days and seeing what happens. During that limited time, you mobilize everything you got and do everything you can to get as many of your followers to buy your product, sign up for your course, join your webinar or visit your homepage as possible. During this particular time window, your goal is to get your followers to see your offer more than once, connect with them, and induce a bit of scarcity if they are not taking action.

When you plan your campaign, whether it's a 3-day, 7-day, or 30-day campaign, you can use this structure:

Step 1: The big reveal

Reveal to your followers that you will launch a product and talk about your product's benefits (not the features).

Step 2: The free taste

Give your followers a peek behind the curtains and give away a free taste.

Step 3: The last chance

Scarcity triggers action, so make sure to communicate when you close the doors. Then, give your followers a last chance to join.

This structure is just a broad framework. For example, if you are doing a 21-day launch, you might spend the first 4-5 days revealing your product, the next 7-10 days to give away a free taste, and the last few days to induce scarcity.

When my friend Marie launched a coaching program to her 600 followers, here is how she planned it:

<u>Week 1</u>

M: Reel - five things I want to create in 2022
T: Stories - Q&A - what do you want to create in 2022?
W: Feed post – Selfie
T: Multi slide feed post - 5 tips that helped me do X
F: Stories - yes/no questions to your Tribe
S: n/a
S: Stories: sharing other accounts

<u>Week 2</u>

M: Reel - try this if you want to accomplish X
T: Stories – entertaining
W: Feed post - share your favorite quote, ask your followers for theirs
T: Multi slide feed post - 5 myths about X

F: Stories - book recommendations
S: n/a
S: Stories: sharing the last time you learned something

<u>Week 3</u>

M: Reel - 8 days left to launch

T: Stories - share testimonials etc

W: Selfie post - share why you are doing this (your story)

T: Multi slide feed post - "the best way to do X."

F: Stories - Q&A "how would your life change if you accomplished X?"

S: Feed: Share something personal

S: Stories: 48hr to launch!

<u>Week 4</u>

M: Reel - 24 to launch

T: Stories - Open! Join now!

W: n/a

T: Multi slide feed post - "talk about how your product solves a real problem."

F: Stories - Closing soon, more free tastes

S: Live video: Keep mentioning the benefits of your product + live Q & A

S: Stories: Last call!

Ways to Monetize

IG offers a multitude of ways to make money. The most common ones are selling your own product or service, affiliate marketing, or subscriptions. I know solo entrepreneurs and small businesses in all these fields, and from my experience, high ticket offers the most profitable products to sell on IG. That being said, you might find success with affiliate marketing, so it's always best to test what works for you. So let's look at how to monetize your IG account in different ways.

How to write a money-making bio

Your IG bio is very important and can be a determining factor if your followers end up buying from you, as well as for whether you get new followers or not. More than your photo, you have your username, 150 characters to describe yourself and/or your business, space for a URL link, and space for a series of highlights.

When it comes to the username, you should try to be as clear as possible. For example, I have the IG name @inkomstmedbocker (translated into English, it becomes @incomewithbooks). Pretty clear what my account is about, right? If the followers immediately get a feel for what your account is about just by reading your username, you have won a lot. Then you can use your profile picture and the 150 characters to connect to them even more deeply without wasting time explaining what your account is about.

As an example, this is how my bio looks:

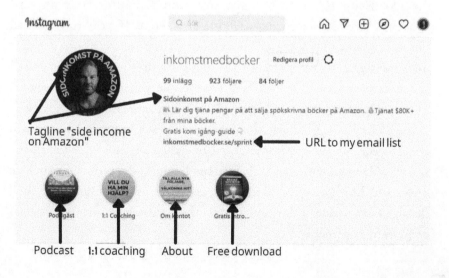

The purpose of my bio-text is to get more followers, but above all, it is to get traffic to my website with the hope of getting more email subscribers, which is in line with my business funnel.

Highlights in the bio

You can include highlights from stories in your bio. I see this a bit like a menu bar on a website. For example, I have an "about" highlight, a highlight about the coaching programs I sell, one about podcasts I've been to, and finally, a highlight to my lead magnet. I do not know if the highlights contribute to more followers and increased sales. Still, in any case, it gives you the chance to provide your followers with an even better picture of who you are or what your company is about, so I recommend you take advantage of that.

Selling low price products on IG

You can make money by selling physical products or digital downloads on IG. If you're an artist, you can offer your physical products (artwork, records, merchandise, etc.). If you run a small business, you can sell digital downloads of reports or eBooks. From my experience, mainly talking to authors, it's pretty damn hard to sell low-price items on IG. I know a few people with a ton of followers (25k+) who struggle to sell even a handful of units. I don't know why that is, but I would advise you not to only sell low-priced items on IG. If you run an e-commerce store, you can use IG as a traffic source and make money that way. That being said, companies such as Stella and Dot (jewelry), Scentsy (scented items), and Jamberry (nail decals) have made a fortune selling their products through IG, so everything is possible.

Affiliate Marketing on IG

If you have an already well-established following on IG, promoting affiliate products is one way to make money. I know a guy in the personal finance space. He made $12,000 in affiliate commissions in 2021 from around 10k followers. He finds his affiliate products on sites like Adrecord, and he's promoting investment bank accounts. Making money on affiliate commissions is not easy because you often need a large following, and you are most likely promoting the same affiliate products as many others IG accounts. In my opinion, if you are only promoting affiliate products, you are leaving a ton of money on the table. Big money on IG will come from selling your own product or service.

Premium Content Subscription

Some people sell access to their premium stories as a subscription service. This is similar to Patreon, in that subscribers pay a monthly fee to gain access to their content. To be successful, you need a large following and valuable content. I know a guy, also in the personal finance space, who shares all the stocks he buys/sells and shares his thoughts about the stock market. He started his premium stories in July 2021. He had 18k IG followers, and 100 people signed up the first month. He kept talking about his premium service every day (marketing rule of seven), and at the end of 2021, 550 people had signed up. He charges $10/month, so that's a $5,500/month IG income right there. I like to compare this type of income to the early stages of launching a podcast or YouTube channel. While you won't make much money at first, your audience will grow over time, and you can make exponentially more money. Think about if you have anything to package and sell like a subscription service.

Create Your Product or service

This is my favorite way of making money on IG! I have talked repeatedly about how important it is to know your followers, and when you do, you can create a product or service they will love. A typical product is to create some kind of course.

Sales tool: How to master your sales calls

When people schedule a call with you, they're taking time out of their day to see what you have to offer. So prepare ahead and make it worth their time. Lead the conversation. That way, you know what to say and how to tackle the questions you get. Here's how to do it.

Set the Agenda

Set the agenda. This will help keep your call on track. Do this by breaking the agenda up into three parts.

First, build connection and ask questions like "why did you reach out to me?", "what are the results you are looking for?", "why is that important to you?"

When you have a bit of background, and a better feel for why they wanted to jump on a sales call with you, keep digging to find out if they have tried to solve their "problem" in any other way before. Ask, "have you tried to [instert the result they want] before?" if they say yes, ask in what way and keep digging. If they say no, ask, "what do you think is your biggest challenge to reach [result]?".

Then, circle back to what you have heard and position your product as the solution to their problem (if it's a good fit!), and talk about the benefits of using your product. Ask if they want to buy your product/ book a session, and keep talking about the benefits they will experience for using your product. Finally, you can share details about how it works behind the scenes, arrange the payments and thank them for their time.

Final reflections about making money on IG

A couple of years ago, when I was completely new to online business, I watched a Youtube video about how important it is to have the right mindset to succeed in business. In that clip, I clearly remember that they said that your business is a mirror image of yourself. I never really understood what that meant back then, but now I do.

In a way, entrepreneurship is a bit like disguised self-development. It is difficult, or almost impossible, to build a successful business without working on yourself, your habits, fears, etc.

Imagine that you feel it's scary to start with video on IG, but you know that video connects much better than regular posts and that video is what will be required if you want to maximize your chances of making money. How do you go about starting with video? You work with your fears, and you take small steps forward until one day when you are confident of recording a video and posting it online. In this way, the development of your business is a direct mirror image of the way you are developing yourself.

You will face many uncomfortable things as soon as you start seeing IG as an income stream. It's easy to get carried away and drawn into what everyone else is doing, how well everyone else is editing their posts, and how many followers everyone else seems to have. To not be affected by what everyone else does, you need to work on yourself and learn how to care less about what people think and feel about you. Your work with yourself will spill over into your business, and you will notice how you constantly need to learn more about yourself to make money on IG.

Now, put yourselves out there and start treating IG like an income stream!

Book 2: Likes Don't Pay Bills: How to Leverage Social Media to Get Leads and Customers

Introduction

Your customers are on social media. They are probably scrolling their feeds right now, as you are reading this. How can I know that? Because *everyone's* customers are on social media all the time.

With the right strategies, you can get their attention, connect with them, and build relationships with them. However, with the wrong strategies, they will scroll right past your posts, and your attempt to use social media as a marketing tool can be a frustrating time-sink.

This book will discuss the many strategies involved in using social media to get leads, customers, and sales. The first part of the book talks about the five biggest myths surrounding social media marketing and what to do instead. The second part of the book teaches you copywriting and email marketing, which are essential skills in the online marketing world.

After you have read this book, you will have all you need to leverage social media to build your platform and get tons of warm leads and turn them into customers for life.

Let's jump right in and start with social media marketing myth #1!

Social Media Marketing Myth 1: Your Followers Care about You

As the number of followers increases, it is easy to get caught up and think that they really care about you. They like your posts after all. This illusion that just because someone hits "like" on your post, they actually like *you* can be very dangerous to some.

Imagine a teenage girl posting makeup tips. The more likes and shares that she has, the more she may believe in the value of the system itself. She may even associate her own value and worth on the number of likes. Do the people who watch her videos actually care about her as a person? Unfortunately, probably not.

The truth is that most followers don't care about you or your posts. It just so happens that your post came across in their feed as they scroll catatonically through countless other posts, ads, and messages.

Although many people are using social media to promote a business or bring awareness to something, there are others who just post for the sake of posting. Do you think that their followers actually care about them? Did they stir some type of emotion in the followers?

So, if we know that your followers do not naturally care about you, the question is how do we make them care? It does sound fairly easy but consider how do we get people to actually care about us in the real world? How do you create an emotional bond with someone with whom you seemingly have nothing in common with?

Sending a Message to Your Followers

Let's start with the basics. What does it really mean for people to care about you? By definition, the word caring means to display kindness and concern for others. It is showing empathy and feelings of compassion for another person. It is touching a person in an emotional way that makes them want to or be willing to inconvenience themselves for your benefit.

We all meet random people every day. But there is no emotional bond established with each and every one of these. There is no possible way for a celebrity like Selena Gomez to have an emotional connection with each and every one of the 100+ million followers through daily, regular, generic posts.

However, if your message is able to meet a person where they are at, touching him or her through your words, pictures and actions, you will be able to create that bond and emotional connection. You have to hit them deep. Reach them in a way that they never expected. Communicate your message in such a way as to express your understanding of their hopes, fears and dreams. Allow them to use their imagination about your relationship and define it as if it is real.

If you are creating posts and messages that appeal to YOU as if you are the audience, then you probably have misread who your audience is and what they really want. Do your research. Determine who it is that you are speaking to, who you want to reach and what is it that they are hoping to receive from you. This is where the value in your message will lie. Take the extra time to research, use the vocabulary of those you are speaking to. Address the real pain points and in fact, be real!

Going back to the celebrities who have a large following. Each of them shares their real stories, and their real struggles with those who want to know. Selena Gomez for example shares her personal struggles with relationships and her career. She engages her followers and lets them know that she understands their struggles too. She shares that her success has come after trials and hardships. She is not simply posting random pictures and posts about unnecessary topics.

Let your audience project their own fantasies towards your message as well.

Learning What Makes People Tick

Great marketing is mostly about learning exactly what people care about: what makes them tick. We know that people do not really care about you when they are looking up to your service. They care about themselves, and how you may help them solve a certain problem. But in most cases, there is more to that.

People will say all kinds of nice things – but in most cases, it is all a façade. Nowadays, the average customer is well-researched, and, likely, they have already gone through countless of your competitors before they got up to you. This is why they will analyze you based on various other circumstances. The trick here is to figure out exactly what makes them tick – what they care about. Here is how you can figure that out:

- **Identify Their Problems**

When you sell a product to a client, you are not selling them a product that you just want to bring into the world: you sell a product that you believe will make their lives easier. You can't sell a customer a product unless it improves their life – it's impractical, yet many business owners put themselves into this situation.

To find out what makes your audience tick, you need to understand who they are – and specifically, what pains they have. Your purpose here is to create a product that may alleviate that pain. Otherwise, you won't be able to get your business going.

Many small business owners are struggling to get out in the world by creating a product, and then present it to a wide audience, hoping that they can attract the right people – but in the meantime, they end up forgetting who their audience is. They are so focused on attracting potential customers that they no longer remember who they are trying to reach. They don't have their pains in mind – but a general product that might solve a certain widespread problem.

This is why, in order to connect with your audience, you need to go to the places that they currently are – no matter if it's in a physical place or a social media one. Try to talk to them regularly and learn about any problems that they might have. Look at reviews and complaints about similar products – see what their actual desires are. This way, you can create better products that you may launch at the right audience.

- **Mind the Vocabulary**

Your followers do not particularly care about you. In fact, they just care about what you say, and how your words are resonating with whatever they have in mind. They care about the way you speak, how your words connect to them.

Whenever you are speaking, not only do you have to be clear in the words that you are using, but you should also use a language that seems attractive to them. A lawyer will not attract potential customers by using the "ghetto language" – they will want to seem as professional as possible. In this case, they might want to use a few "fancy" words that will help deliver an image.

At the same time, if your audience is formed out of people such as students or stay-at-home mothers, then you might want to refrain from the extra professional language. Your fancy, pompous words will not phase them in the way that you are hoping – and in truth, it might just send them in a different direction. People are looking for the kind of language and behavior that they can connect to, not the kind that will ascertain your show-off qualities.

Bear in mind that your vocabulary should also contain "trigger words" – or as marketers refer to them, "words that sell." Certain words in your vocabulary may attract customers to your side, keeping them there with certain words that sell. They may not realize it themselves, but words such as "you," "new," or even something as simple as "tips" may earn you quite a few followers. This is because you can manage to connect to them on a deeper level – as long as you also learn how to steer clear of clichés.

The same thing goes with the vocabulary that your potential customer is using. What words are they using? Do they seem like they are trying to convey something to you? What words are they using specifically – and do they mostly consist of positive or negative words? Do they seem to be using a lot of "mhm" words or short monosyllabic responses? If that is the case, even if they are your followers or not, it is likely that you will not be able to hang on to them for very long.

By lending an ear at the words that your potential customers are using, you will be able to figure out exactly what makes them tick. What do they seem to be interested in? What exactly does it seem particularly boring to them? The richer their vocabulary, the more they might be interested in what you have to sell them. Your tone of voice will also be quite determinant, as they will be looking for someone with a calm attitude – not someone that will rush them into taking action.

- **Pay Attention to the Body Language**

When you are talking with a customer, you should pay attention to your body language and the body language of your client. Specifically, you might want to focus on the feedback that your customer is giving you – although this mostly applies to when you are speaking with the customer face to face.

Most of the advice that we receive in concerns to feedback focuses on the things that we have to say – but the non-verbal communication is very important as well. For example, by conveying discomfort or aggression using your body language, you might end up making them feel unsafe – therefore, preventing them from further listening to what you have to say. Sometimes, it's the little gestures that give away the way they feel – and all you have to do is "listen" to what their body language is telling you. If they do not feel a connection to what you are trying to convey to them through your body language, then you might just lose them in the long run.

Myth 2: More Likes and Shares are Better

We all love that feeling when you post something on Facebook or Instagram and you watch the number of LIKES go up. You feel accomplished as the volume of shares increases by the minute and you know that more and more people are viewing your message. We tend to feel better about ourselves and the message we are trying to spread as we watch the likes and shares increase.

We want the message to go viral, thinking that will increase our popularity and in turn, our money. The myth that the more likes that you have the more famous or rich you will be is simply that, a myth and will hurt your opportunities to truly be famous or rich if you let it.

In reality, likes won't pay your bills or put food on the table. The algorithms that sites like Facebook and Instagram utilize will certainly spread your message far and wide, but for what purpose. Is the number of likes truly an indicator of the success of your social media marketing?

The Marketing Measurements

As it is said, what gets measured gets done. In the case of social media marketing, what gets measured, gets the attention. The number of likes simply shows the popularity of the fan page. It does not necessarily indicate that the follower will go out and purchase the product. It displays brand awareness and knowledge. Or simply that the particular ad was attractive or appealing.

At the end of 2017, Buffer.com conducted a study of posts, which were the highest ranking for the year. A post by a photographer who had created a warped view of the world reached more than 803,000 people, was shared 2,300 times and reacted to more than 9K times. However, it did not earn any money. It was simply an engagement post. Kudos to the person who posted it for these very impressive numbers but unfortunately, it did not make this photographer a millionaire.

Another post, about Instagram marketing, received 644 reactions, reached more than 334,000 people and most importantly, was clicked on 34, 372 times. This last number is an indication that not only did viewers see the ad, but it was of interest to them and they wanted to learn more. This emotional response triggered an action. The advertiser struck a nerve, prompting more than 34K people to follow the link and engage.

This reaction, prompting an action is the key to your social media marketing. It is not the advertisement itself that will bring in the revenue, but instead the emotional response that you will incite in your potential client. That emotion, feeling or interest is what will prompt them to take action.

Consider the infamous commercials during the Half Time Show at the Super Bowl. People everywhere are at parties, the local bar or on the couch waiting with baited breath to see what the creative will put out there for your viewing pleasure. In the coffee room the next morning, the conversation typically revolves around the best and of course, worst commercials. The discussion probably swirls around the commercials even more so than the game itself. It would be an interesting study to review and evaluate the conversation surrounding both the best and worst to see which product is actually identified with each commercial. I would be willing to bet that most people could not tell you. Although they LIKED the funny commercial with the old guy, they have no idea what product it was for. The heart-wrenching ad with the kittens may have tugged at your heartstrings, but will it make you immediately go out to buy whatever it is they are selling? Probably not.

As you can see, just because someone LIKES or even shares your post or your ad, you are simply generating awareness. A person is acknowledging in a way that he/she SAW it but then quickly moves on to the next one in the news feed. Imagine scrolling down through your posts and just hitting LIKE for each and every one. Did you actually read everyone's posts? Do you understand the message that each of your friend's was trying to share? What if they asked you about it later, could you tell them what it said? Probably not. You simply acknowledged that they were active on the site and kept moving. Don't forget, there are a lot of posts to read!

The bottom line is this…is the number of likes really the best measurement of a successful post or campaign? A better way to measure is to evaluate what type of chain reaction you can begin with your posts. How many people have shared your message or talked about it with others?

Don't try to be all things to all people. Some entrepreneurs and business owners try to connect with and cater to all people. This strategy, not really a strategy at all, will diminish the value of your product and the market that you should be targeting to.

Draw a line in the sand. Figure out who in fact you should be targeting to and make a stand. Research the actual likes and dislikes of this demographic of people and focus your marketing strategy on providing them with the appropriate material to solicit an emotional response.

How will this impact you and your business you may be asking? By targeting those people with whom you can connect, you have a much better chance of them converting to an actual customer rather than simply clicking LIKE. This deceptive number or perception of popularity is still necessary but to truly gauge the value of your marketing, the number of sales that occurred as a result of your campaign is a much better measure.

Likes are the end result of a temporary feeling about your campaign. To successfully impact change and long-term sales and customers, you must focus of creating a strategy and content that will stand the test of time. In your efforts, you are looking to develop a brand that will be recognizable, memorable and longstanding.

I am sure you are familiar with many brands that have been able to endure throughout the years, amidst competition, varying promotional strategies and even challenges within the company itself. Companies like Levi Strauss, Colgate-Palmolive, Mercedes-Benz, Kraft, The New York Times and Tiffany & Co. have not only been able to endure and survive but actually come out on top.

Although times have changed and in fact, the markets may have changed, each of these companies has researched the target audience and tailored their marketing campaigns towards specific individuals with specific qualities and needs. This strategy has been used no matter whether the campaign was in print, billboard, or social media.

Just because Mercedes-Benz may have placed an amazing, historic commercial on the Super Bowl one year, and it was the topic of conversation the next day, that does not mean that the intended audience was EVERYONE who was watching at the time. The campaign was geared towards a certain type of person watching the game at the time; only that engagement will turn into a sale. It wasn't that the commercial was talked about or LIKED that made it an effective campaign. It was instead the number of people who felt a deeper connection with the message in the commercial; those who now felt that their desires, dreams and emotions were engaged and connected to are the ones who went out and in fact, purchased a Mercedes-Benz.

How will you engage your target audience?

Quality vs. Quantity – How to Make Sure You Get Quality

Some people focus a lot on the quantity of the product rather than on the quality. "The more, the merrier" – or this is how the saying generally goes. The problem is that if you wish for your marketing to be successful, you may want to focus on quality instead – because this is what matters.

In truth, both quality and quantity are important – buy you will need to create the right balance for both of them. For instance, let's say that you create a lot of posts every week, and you have quite a number of followers that like or share your product – but no one really buys it. So, while the product may seem to have potential, you haven't gone high enough to get profit.

On the other hand, if you create good quality content, it will be much easier for the followers to connect with what you have to say. Once

73

they get engaged in your high-quality content, there is a high chance that this will also result in conversion. The more they stay on your website, the higher the chances are that they will buy something – and this can only happen if you create content that is attractive for the visitors.

The Question of "What to Measure"

So, what should you measure instead, if quantity is not something that you should put your trust in? Most people measure the likes that you get on a post – and in a way, it's good – because it gives you a good idea of how many people are interacting with your website.

But hear this: not every person that hits "like" on your post will access the link to your article/page. A lot of people will see the title, possibly agree with it, and then hit the like button as a reflex. Some may even access your post – but once they see that the quality of your post is not enough to keep them interested, they will hit "back" on that website as soon as they entered it. This will not help your website traffic much – in fact, it will only bring it down.

To make potential followers stick to your website, you need to create content that they will enjoy reading – that will give them enough reason to stay on your website for as long as it is needed to go through anything. The more they stay there, the higher the chances will be that search engines will pick on to this – deeming you as a quality website and putting you higher up the ranks.

The purpose of your post is not to get likes; everyone can get those. Nowadays, you can simply purchase those likes off the Internet – through accounts that deliver those likes to you. You can get the likes, which will make your post seem more popular – but in truth, there won't be many conversions for you there. You will need people to come in contact with your website – to get you the traffic that you deserve.

This is why instead of focusing on the likes that you get, you should focus on the traffic that your website receives. How many visitors do you get on your website on a daily basis? How much time do those people spend on your website? Do they stay there for only a few seconds, or do they spend more than a couple of minutes doing research? If they end up spending quite a lot of time there, then it's clear that your content brings them quite a lot of good information.

With each post, you are hoping to get new readers – readers that can benefit from your information. You want to help them make the right choice and inform them about the purchases that they want to make – give them all the details so that in the end, they pick you. This is why it does not make sense to focus on the likes when you need to keep them on board.

Your goal here is to measure the traffic and improve it if it's not working how you are hoping. Remember, your goal here is to get your traffic and obtain conversion – which is why you should spend less attention on the likes and more on the actual traffic.

Myth 3: There Is So Much Noise, I Need to Find the Best Hack to Break Through

Noise, or things that are a distraction or not useful to you, are plentiful on social media. You are constantly hit with spam, junk email, ads for things you never knew you had searched for or even needed and even those cute little puppies. Your inbox is full of useless content and your feed is clogged with distractions.

Most people try to develop tactics to break through the noise and there are various things that have been tried. One strategy is to trick people into action. Unfortunately, this is a shortsighted strategy that focuses only on something you cannot control – those things that show up in feeds.

Instead of trying to trick people into clicking, your strategy should focus on connecting with people and bringing the discussion outside of social media. Yes. I said it. The horror! In our highly digital, technology driven world, most people cannot live a minute without their phone in their hand. They go to sleep scrolling and swiping right or left. They wake up to the alarm on their phone and before even setting foot out of the bed, they have checked email and Facebook for any new information.

The connection that you want to create to sidestep this concept of noise is to initiate a conversation online but have it continue outside of the virtual space – in the real world! You want people to be talking about it, sharing it, and yes, even dancing to it. Just like the wildly popular Gangnam Style.

Released in 2012, it became the first video on YouTube to hit 2 BILLION views. Yes, that's right! We are talking billions here! Not only were followers watching this soon to be famous video, but they were in fact sharing, liking and DOING the Gangnam style dance moves. Soon after, the artist, Psy, was accused of stealing some of his dance moves from another artist, causing controversy and of course, more discussion. Now everyone wanted to not only watch this Korean guy dance and sing, they wanted to compare it to another group's moves. The more discussion, the more traffic to the website, the more views and shares.

How does this translate to earnings? Although viewers watch videos on YouTube for free, the advertising that is displayed on the page is the revenue generator. As more and more people watched this amazing video, the more people who would see the ads, click and ultimately purchase something. According to Google's Chief Business officer, Psy's video brought in more than $8 million strictly through viewers on YouTube.

It was not a matter of how many followers Psy had or even how many people actually like him or his style. It was the conversations, the controversy and the fact that everyone needed to see what the hype was all about that drew the traffic to his video. He was able to break through the noise to create a winning product. Psy was not just another guy on the internet sharing his music. Between July and September of 2012, through word of mouth, Gangnam Style very quickly ascended the ranks of top videos and in this short time, had been viewed more than 2 million times. As the dance began to catch on, people began to record themselves dancing the Gangnam Style and posting on YouTube. This brought in additional views for Psy as viewers compared their dance to the original.

As the video began to go viral, it caught the attention of the media. Rather than Psy having to approach the media about his video to promote it and drive traffic, they were coming to HIM. The more press he received, the more traffic was driven to his video. What a truly amazing marketing campaign in which he really did not have to do much. What he did do was start a conversation in the social media landscape, which led to conversations *outside* social media. Through his music, he targeted a very specific group of people who he knew would want to listen to new, fresh music and would easily share and talk about his work.

This is how Psy broke through the noise and how you can too. It will require research and effort but, in the end, you will reap the benefits by having your products or services talked about outside of social media.

Of course, the first thing that you must do is identify your target market. Who are you selling to? What product or service will solve a problem that this particular group is interested in? Do your research and learn all that you can about this market.

Whether you start out with a following 100 or 1,000, you need to actively listen to what your audience is telling you; what do they like; what topics are regularly discussed. Utilize analytics to determine what it is they are talking about, what they react to and what posts and topics get the most attention. Listening is the first step towards writing great content that will stir a reaction in your intended audience. This emotional reaction will be the trigger for them to begin the conversation.

Through your content, you want to make your audience believe that they are important to you. Be relatable and transparent. You are not trying to trick anyone into buying or sharing information. Be your genuine self both on and offline by sharing your desire to help, influence or provide them with a benefit. When you speak to and connect with people on a level that is personal and non-salesy, you conquer the noise and develop an unbreakable bond.

In the marketing of Gangnam Style, we can only imagine what Psy's strategy was to market to his audience. His passion for music was evident in the video through his facial expressions and dance moves and he shared his love with his audience. This came through as a feel-good reaction which viewers just felt compelled to share with others. He connected with his audience on a deeper level than simply a new, upbeat song. He caused that emotional reaction that you should also be trying to obtain from you viewers, willing them to share it with others.

By getting to know your target audience, you can create great content about things that are important to them and about things that will help them create a better life. Pictures also speak a thousand words. When considering what will touch a person emotionally and will spark that further discussion, consider what visually sparks your interest. What pictures on Instagram make you pause your scrolling to look more carefully at it? What images take your breath away and then encourage you to show it to a friend or family member? Maybe it stirs an emotion that prompts a discussion.

This same emotion that is stirred within you is what you want to bring out for your followers. You want to use photos that will not only speak a thousand words to them but that they will in turn, speak a thousand words about. Your audience is the best promotion that you could ask for when the conversation is taken out of social media and into the real world. Inevitably, those that they talk about it with will come back to social media to see it for themselves or to join the online conversation.

Through your outstanding message and content, you can take a small group of diligent and faithful followers and turn them into your marketing army. By consistently sharing the same message, you establish yourself as reliable, trustworthy and knowledgeable. People will see you as someone who cares about their needs which will in turn, build your reputation and encourage them to discuss and share.

Consider the local motivational speaker who regularly posts inspirational and motivational content. He knows what it is that his followers want and what they react to. His content continuously creates an emotional response within each and every person that it touches. His message is shared countless numbers of times on social media and discussed between friends. New followers seek out his websites to hear his inspiring words for themselves. His message is no longer simply another of the many inspiring messages that pass through the news feed, adding to the social media noise. They have instead become sought after, daily nuggets of affirmation. Each and every follower feels the connection with the speaker as if they are personal friends, and the valuable feelings that go with it.

Myth 4: Post X Times per Day at Exactly X O'clock

I have to post every day at the same time to ensure that my audience is available and ready to receive my message. NOT!

When it comes to social media marketing, we tend to focus on how many times per day and what time we post. This strategy assumes that people only check their social media feeds at certain times and does not take into account the other more important factors.

If you have done your research, you will already understand that when people are interested in a particular topic, they will follow and view your content. By connecting with your small group of followers, your targeted audience, you can be assured that they will see it. They want to see it and if you are being consistent, with powerful and fulfilling content, they will seek it out no matter what time of day or what day of the week you post it.

Studies of trends in social media originally suggested that to reach the maximum number of followers and to increase your engagement, you had to post during commuting time, lunch and break times, and evenings. This slightly outdated information has not been updated with new trends and to cover unique target groups.

Rather than focusing on the specific times and days that you should be posting, instead focus on what works best for YOUR followers. By having an understanding of the habits and social media routines of your audience, you can better determine what will be the best time to post to gain the most exposure for your content.

The key here is for YOUR content. Each target market or audience will have its own best time to post. For example, if you are targeting moms of young children, you can be pretty sure that rush hour and mid-afternoon will NOT be appropriate times to post content. They will be too busy getting kids on and off the bus or to and from school to notice your post. However, if you post at 9pm, you might be more likely to get their attention after the children are settled in for the night and finally get some "me" time to scroll through social media. It may even be their guilty pleasure for the day, the only time they have to read something that interests them. Because this may be a similar time for others as well, they may not only see it, but share it and then chat about it at tomorrow's PTA meeting since it will be fresh in their minds.

On the other hand, if you are promoting a new deli that has just opened up in town, you may want to post and share mouth-watering pictures of the delicacies that you offer at 11am each day. You can be pretty sure that people will be searching for lunch options around this time and what better time to engage not only their senses but their stomachs as well. If they then come in to purchase lunch from your deli, you can now establish a deeper connection in person, encouraging them to start a conversation off of social media as well with others to stop in and enjoy your food.

When it comes to social media, of course, your goal should be to gain the most engagement within the first few hours of posting. Studies

82

have shown that the likelihood of your post being seen decreases as the time goes on. Going back to the deli, it would not be a good idea to post about your new lunch specials AFTER the lunch rush. At that point, you would simply be adding to the social media noise as your followers scroll past your post on their way to find something else that interests them.

Have you ever heard your friend say "did you see Jane's post last week?" Unless you saw it shortly after Jane posted it, it is highly possible that the noise in your social media feed has overpowered Jane's post and it is no longer visible or even relevant any longer. That being said, you need to capitalize on the momentum of engagement and not only post but engage with your audience while they are available.

If you recall, earlier in this book we discussed proactively connecting with and reactively connecting with your audience. By interacting with them during this time after you post, you are reinforcing your concern for them and their importance to you. As you receive comments on your posts, be sure to respond as soon as possible.

However, we have also seen that trends have changed as many people pick up their phones to mindlessly scroll through their social media feeds before they even set foot out of bed. So, in reality, no matter what time of day, or how many times you post, either your followers will see it or they won't. There is no perfect time or pre-determined number of times per week that contains the magic number to guarantee that followers will see it and engage.

Instead, focus on producing great content and posting regularly, whatever that means to you. Maybe it is once per day or once per week, but create a regular schedule of posting so that your followers will look forward to receiving your engaging content at that particular time. By consistently posting amazing content, you will automatically draw people in as loyal followers who are willing to share and discuss with their friends.

Another problem with social media posting is the actual algorithms that are behind the scenes running the show. Have you ever wondered how it is that they know that you recently searched for a place to take a new yoga class? The algorithms and science behind social media pick up on your trends, your searches and views and will automatically send you posts and advertisements that coincide with these. It is as if Big Brother is truly watching – hello *1984*! George Orwell's prophetic book, written in 1948, describes a society in the future in, which all citizens are watched. It does make you feel like someone is watching when suddenly you see these ads for something that you were recently looking for pop up on your screen. But this is how the algorithm's work and they change. However, you cannot plan your post timing based on these or any assumptions that your content will automatically get shared to someone who was searching for it.

Finding your exact social media sweet spot is overrated. There is no such thing as the perfect time to post or the magic formula for the right combination of when and how many times to post. People check their social media posts all of the time so they will at some point see your posts. The key to success stems from focusing your content and posts on what is important for your audience, tailoring your message to truly what will impact your followers and spark that emotional response. So, no matter what time you choose to post, make sure your message is consistent, relevant and emotionally charged. The sweet spot will lie there right in your hands.

Myth 5: My Product Doesn't Sell – Fix It with More Ads

My product isn't selling, it must be that I am not advertising it enough. I will fix it by placing more ads online. Really? Just because Facebook is telling you that you should Boost your post, doesn't mean that is the best way to go. It is no guarantee though that just because you spend the money to advertise that you will in fact reap any return on your investment at all.

It is very common for business owners, especially new entrepreneurs, to consider social media ad campaigns as the cure-all solution for selling a product or building a following. Many people believe that as long as we spend money on advertising, everything will work out just fine. I am not saying that paid advertising is not necessarily required. What I am saying is that it will not solve all of your problems or drive traffic to your website. It is by far a quick fix!

Let's look at a small non-profit organization looking to drive traffic to their website with the hope that people will see value in the services offered, the lives they impact and they will be moved to donate to the cause. The organization has a $1000 budget for the year for advertising expenses and they believe that their $1000 should convert to possibly thousands of dollars in donation revenue. Unfortunately for them, even with their good intentions, the ads have not driven the traffic to their website nor earned them any significant money in donations.

On its own, the non-profit's website does not convert followers to philanthropists so executives sought for a magic solution to their problem, thinking that social media ads were going to be their golden egg. Sadly, after spending too much money on ads, the organization received no donations at all.

Then there are of course those companies who do virtually no advertising, yet seem to come out on top. The fashion retailer, Zara, carefully studies their customers' desires and listens to what they want. Information is sent back to the design team daily, sharing what it is customers are looking for. This ingenious way of design development and producing what it is the customers want has inspired customers to share through word of mouth this incredible process. No advertising required!

Companies whose main objective is to meet a need will find that very little advertising is required. Each of the following companies followed several similar tactics in their marketing strategy instead of advertising and as you will see, they all have come out on top:

Costco, the second largest retailer in the world, does not do any advertising. By getting to know their customers first, they were able to achieve their success by customers sharing their amazing experiences in the store by word of mouth.

With products geared towards the adrenaline-junkie, GoPro established its presence in the market through its online videos, which depict other adventure seekers in action. The founders researched their target market and just knew that those who are on the constant search for the adrenaline rush would not be able to resist sharing the amazing stunts and feats that their fellow junkies had recorded. Thrill-seekers around the world shared information about the videos and camera products, building a community of others videotaping their own outdoor adventures. No advertising needed!

The award winning product produced by Tesla requires no fancy ads for you to know what it is. Executives at Tesla rely on the quality of their electric vehicle and the surge in environmental concern to propel the company's sales without spending a dollar on advertising. See for yourself how people talk after one of these high-tech, sleek vehicles passes them on the highway.

Word spreads like wildfire when someone has experienced excellent service, found a great product or feels important and respected. On the other hand, word of mouth can work against you as well. Have you ever had a poor experience at a restaurant and very quickly posted a negative review about your experience? People searching for a new restaurant read these reviews and they can weigh very heavily on someone's choice to dine there or not. As much as word of mouth is a good thing, it can also work against you if you have not ensured you meet all of the customers' requirements and needs.

The online retailer, Zappos, was built with word-of-mouth as their only marketing strategy. Spending their advertising budget instead on customer service, they have become one of the largest online retailers of clothing and shoes. Their strategy of excellent customer service has driven repeat business while word-of-mouth has continued to bring in new customers to experience it as well.

For each of these companies, there was, in fact, a formula to their success, which you can apply to your products and services as well.

We will discuss in more detail in the next chapter how to use social media properly to help you attain the results you are looking for.

Part II - How to Use Social Media to Build Your Platform

In this day and age, if anyone ever thinks about social media marketing, one big platform comes to mind – Facebook. With the billions of users currently on that platform, it feels like the best place to market your offer, right? And if you think about it, the idea is quite sound. Think about the number of eyeballs your posts can get – and it is more likely that people will see you in a Facebook post rather than in a Google search. With today's use of social media, most people log onto Facebook every few minutes, scroll for a bit, laugh at a few memes – and in the meantime, see a few ads and posts. You don't see them going on Google for these things.

However, here's a thought: what if, one day, Facebook would cease to exist? One day, Mark Zuckerberg decided that he no longer wanted to go with Facebook. What if Facebook would slowly go into the background and become a distant memory?

Before you go and say that "that's not possible!" think about MySpace. Think about how popular it used to be before Facebook appeared. Every cool kid and every big business had a MySpace account – and aside from the people who did not know how to use a computer, everyone was connected on MySpace. A few years ago, if you wanted to become successful, you had to start with MySpace.

And there was a business at some point that did precisely that: they conducted all of their marketing moves on MySpace and became immensely popular. People were opting for their services, sharing their content – they were pretty much everywhere on the ads of MySpace. And that was precisely the problem: they were *only* on MySpace and no other platforms.

You can imagine that this was somewhat problematic when MySpace fell through, and the platform failed. A platform that was once so successful suddenly started losing all of its people – all of them migrating to Facebook, Instagram, and all the other "cool websites." The company in question lost all of its followers practically overnight – and they could never recover from the loss. This was simply because they no longer had the clients following them since they put all their faith in MySpace.

I don't want that to happen to you; therefore, I recommend viewing social media as a tool to build your platform. A platform that is yours, a platform you control, so you don't need to depend on the latest social media algorithmic changes or get someone else permission to get your message out there. You can build a platform in many ways, but I highly suggest providing an email list and using social media to grow that list. Email marketing is the number one best sales channel, and we are not going to stop using email anytime soon.

Plus, unlike Facebook and other social media platforms that filter who sees your content, email marketing will let everything go through. You control who sees the subject of your content. Once it goes into the inbox, it is all a matter of whether your follower opens your email or not.

The rest of this book will focus on how you can leverage social media to build a platform that you own. We will start with what to post on social media, move on with social media copywriting tips and end with how to do email marketing like a pro.

Chapter 6 - What and Where to Post on Social Media to Attract Your Target Audience

Your primary aim and ultimate goal with all your social media marketing efforts, regardless of which social media platform you use, should be to get people to sign up for your email list. Why? Because an email list is something that you own. It's yours. That's where the marketing magic is going to happen and you will turn those leads into raving fans and happy customers. I will talk more about email marketing in chapter 8, but first, let's look at where and what to post on social media to get those leads.

Post in Groups

The vast majority of social media interaction has moved away from the public feeds into closed groups. It's estimated that up to 80 percent of all social media chatter occurs in those groups. It doesn't matter if you are doing your marketing on Facebook, LinkedIn, or any other platform. Finding relevant and active groups in your niche is a must. These groups will quickly bring you to your target audience, mainly because most people in those groups share a common interest. Those groups can be pure gold and generate a flood of leads back to you and your business. The strategy for succeeding with group posting (and not being banned from the group) is simple. You slowly build up your authority within the group by posting valuable posts and comments, and step by step, drop more and more backlinks to your site and mention your service more regularly.

Posting on Instagram (feed/stories)

Instagram can be a massive lead generator if your strategy is right. Most people post endless feed-posts about their offers, making their feed look like an advertising page. Don't do that. Save your marketing efforts to your IG stories and treat your feed as a picture wall in your living room. When people visit your IG profile and glance at your feed posts, they should feel about you as a person or you as a company.

If you are using Instagram, make sure to optimize your profile page. Your profile headline is searchable on Google, so include some of your main niche keywords in there. And use the URL box and link back to your email sign-up page as well!

One last note on Instagram: treat Instagram as a tool to grow your business. That means that most of your "IG time" should be spent on creating content for your IG followers, not scrolling your feed.

Paid Social Media ads

I would not recommend paying for advertising if you are new to social media marketing. There are tons of ways to generate traffic for free. If you are more sophisticated and have a budget to spend, go ahead and try paid ads. The general strategy with paid ads, In my opinion, should be to get people to join your email list, but I might be wrong here. I'm not an expert in paid ads (yet), so I encourage you to do your research before starting your ad campaigns.

A note on giveaways

If you have been using Facebook or Instagram, you may have noticed that there are quite a few brands and pages that offer giveaways. "Share this post, tag a friend, and earn a chance to win something" is what most of these posts tend to say. These giveaways are not because the brands are oh-so-generous – it's because it's a good tactic to raise awareness for your brand and grow your following.

Even though this tactic might generate a flood of new followers, how many of them do you think care about you? I can give you a hint - not that many! Giveaways are a great way to get new followers, but most new followers are probably more interested in winning the giveaway than buying your offer. Be careful!

What to Post on Social Media?

We have touched on where to post; now, let's take some time and talk about *what* to post. There are hundreds of things that you may post on social media, all of which are directly related to your business. You need to decide which one works best at this point for your business. By making the right choice, you should increase your brand awareness and get more leads. Here are just a few of the countless ideas that you may post on social media.

- **Before and After Pictures**

Let's say that you are selling a product that would lead to a significant transformation. It may be a new hair dye, a face mask, a weight loss program, or even cabinet paint – whatever leads to a considerable change. To prove its effectiveness and get your leads, you may want to post before and after pictures that will showcase the effect of that product.

The transformation that you are showing may be personal, or it may be related to your business. For example, you may show before and after pictures of your website redesign. Or, if you are a nutritionist, you may post before and after photos of your customer's refrigerator – post-cleaning it. These small things are surely going to get potential customers interested.

- **Behind the Scenes Videos**

Followers are curious by nature, so a good thing to do would be to post behind-the-scenes videos. Share a few pictures of what's happening when working (try to catch the moments when you are going your hardest at it), and get your followers interested. Something good to post would be the location of a project, your office, or a special event that your company is hosting. This will allow customers to connect with you on a personal level.

- **How-to Posts**

How-to posts are also quite popular among followers. Here, you may share a blog post or a video showcasing how to do something specific – but that would also appeal to the ideal customer. Obviously, it should also appeal to your niche.

Let's say, for example, that your business is related to the wedding industry. In this case, you might want to make a post or a video on how to create decorations on a budget – or a photo booth for your wedding reception. You may opt for the help of other people that are skilled in the post creation – but if you use someone else's video, you might want to tag the creator of the video as well. This technique known as back linking might not only help them, but it might also bring clients from their page to yours.

- **Tips Articles**

Time-saving tips, money-saving tips, quick hacks – these types of posts are pretty popular among followers. For example, if you post promotional content about what you are selling, there is a chance that the followers will not click because they are not interested at that point. However, once they see post-market "tips," there's a part of their brain that will "activate" and make them curious.

You might think that giving them tips will not exactly help your product – but somewhere in the back of their minds, your followers will be influenced. For example, let's say that you are selling homemade cleaning solutions. In this case, an article on "tips to clean your house" might seem like it's just giving them general tips – but in truth, it will just make them more interested in cleaning products. This way, you are indirectly influencing them to buy your product.

- **What If I Don't Get Leads?**

If you aren't getting any leads, then it means that the tactic you are currently using is not effective. The campaign you are using might be poorly strategized, the budget might be wrong, or the campaign objective was not very well thought of. If you see that you aren't getting any leads, then you might want to ask yourself the following questions:

- **Am I giving value to my customers?**

You might think that you are selling a fantastic product that can change your customers' lives – but it might only change *your* life and be of no value to others. Think of the ideal customer, create a profile for them – and try to determine exactly who in your area might benefit from this product. You might want to create surveys to learn what the clients want and provide them valuable products.

- **Am I using the right metrics?**

If you aren't getting any leads, the chances are that your current event metrics are not exactly reliable. They may be focused more on the quantity of the contacts that came onto your page rather than on the quality (i.e., vanity metrics), and they are not telling you how many of those contacts are "bouncing." If the metrics are the problem, try shifting your focus to the ones based on the quality.

- **Am I posting the right content?**

Sometimes, the reason for you not getting any leads might be as simple as "your content is not interesting enough." It may be because you are not posting content to your customers' interest (content that might bring them informational value), or it might be that your content is simply boring, confusing, or poorly written. In this case, if the customer is not content with what you are posting, then it is pretty clear that you won't be generating any leads.

If this happens, there are two ways for you to go: first, you might want to try honing your copywriting skills. Learn a few tips and tricks

(I show you how in chapter 8), and if you already have a way with words, this should be easy for you – with a little bit of practice. On the other hand, if you do not have the skills, you might want to hire someone with the necessary knowledge to give you this advantage. In most cases, just a few changes in your marketing campaign should be enough to get you the leads you need. Just figure out what went wrong, and try to correct each pressing matter.

Chapter 7 - How to Get Your Target Markets Attention on Social Media (crash course in copywriting)

Copywriting is the most undervalued skill in marketing. I don't know why, maybe because it's sexier to talk about ad spend and the hottest hashtags of the day? But let's be real here, getting good at copywriting can dramatically improve your overall marketing results and gets you more bang for every marketing unit (time, money, and energy) you invest.

Everything you write on social media is copywriting in one form or another—every single word. The text you include in your Instagram images is copywriting. The text you write in your caption is copywriting. The description on your Youtube video is copywriting. Everything you write is copywriting!

The reason for taking the time to learn how to master copywriting is simple. First, It will force you to look at the world from your audience's point of view. That act in itself is priceless in marketing. As we have talked about through this book, marketing is not about you or your company. Marketing is about *what's in it for your audience.* Why should they care? How will their lives be better? Copywriting pushes you to think about these questions and tailor your message, so it's crystal clear what's in it for them.

The classic copywriting formula AIDA

There are many different formulas for writing copy, and there are many different forms of copy. If you are writing a description for one of your products, that's copy. And if you are writing a Facebook ad for that product, that's copy as well. I highly recommend you take the time to learn the different types of copy you write in your business, but as a starting point, I recommend the classic copywriting formula AIDA. AIDA stands for attention, interest, desire, and action. You can think about AIDA as a general formula and adapt it to your specific needs.

Attention

Step number one is always to get people's attention. If you can't get their attention, well, it will be hard to accomplish anything. How do you get someone's attention on social media? It's not easy these days, but there are a few things you can do. First of all, you need to identify your target market. The words you use, the images you use, everything must be tailored to your target market. Using social media to get leads and customers is not about getting everyone's attention and "breaking through the noise," as we talked about earlier. It's getting the right people's attention. That's all that matters. When you design your images, don't think about what you think "looks good." Think instead about your target market. The same goes for headlines.

Don't write "catchy" headlines for the sake of being catchy. Write headlines that resonate with your audience!

Interest/Desire

So you got your target market's attention, now what? Now it's time to start digging deeper, getting them to listen to what you have to say. This is the trickiest part. If you got their attention but didn't follow up with something interesting, they will most likely leave and never come back.

Let's say you write an attention-grabbing headline and get your ideal customer to start reading your post. What you need to do now to build up interest by sharing something they care about. You can do that by telling a story that resonates with them or talk about anything related to their hopes, fears, and dreams. The trick here is always to think, "what's in it for them? What's in it for them?" It's not about you at this stage; it's about them. It's about their interest, not yours.

When you nail the interest/desire part of your copy, your audience wants MORE. The copy you wrote has aroused them, got their blood pumping, and the dopamine flowing in their bodies. They want more, and they want it NOW.

Do you see how that works? You are not forcing them on anything at this point; you have grabbed their attention and built up their interest. You are almost there; all you need now is not to screw up the action part.

Action

You have probably heard of the term CTA before, which stands for *call to action*. CTAs are super important in copywriting. CTAs are what make people buy your stuff, sign up for your email list, reaching out to you, like your posts (not that important, but it's still an action), and telling their friends about how awesome you are.

A CTA is a prompt, statement, question at the end of your copy that works like an invisible hand that gets people to act on whatever you want them to act upon.

Here's the one thing that most people miss with a good CTA: you can never force someone to do something. An act must come from within; otherwise, it's manipulation. If you have done your job with getting their attention, making them interested in what you have to say, then the CTA doesn't need to be written in bold letters with tons of exclamation marks. All you need to do is to lead them wherever you want them to go.

Many people talk about CTA as if it's all that matters, but they are wrong. A CTA itself can rarely do all the heavy lifting. You as the marketer must get your prospects' attention, take them on a journey in your interest/desire phase and leave them with the decision of acting on your CTA. If you have done your job right, they will almost always act on the CTA. The key here (again) is to be authentic and know your audience, focusing on them and always ask yourself, "what's in it for them."

How to always have something to post

Coming up with new content is not that hard. When you are using the AIDA formula and focus on your target audience, you will get a TON of engagement on your posts. People will ask all kinds of questions, reach out to you to share their stories, and always provide you with new material. The trick to never run off of things to say is to listen to what your market is telling you, create a piece of content about that, and repeat the process.

One last note on copy

I have talked about the general frame you can use when writing your posts, ads, emails, and more. I have specifically not written his chapter with many plug-and-play templates simply because you have to develop your voice in your copy. The AIDA formula will get you here, even if it might require some experimentation.

Chapter 8. How to Use Social Media to Get Email Subscribers

How to get quality email subscribers

Step number one in getting started with email marketing (aside from the technical stuff) is to get people to sign up for your email list. That might sound simple, but it's not. An email list of people who want to hear from you is the most valuable asset any marketer can have. What makes it so valuable is the level of effort it takes for people to sign up in the first place. Most people hold on to their email addresses with all they got these days, asking questions: Is this valuable? Do I want his/her emails? What credentials do they have? The million-dollar question is always *how do I get more quality people to sign up for my list?!* Before I tell you how to do that, I will explain the differences between building an email list and providing an email list.

Building vs. providing an email list

You are probably familiar with the expression building an email list. I don't have anything against that; I'm a huge believer in email marketing. What I don't like is phrase *building*. I think a better way to view an email list is something you are *providing*. Let's discuss the difference.

When we talk about building an email list, it's easy to fall into the trap of the numbers game and only focus on getting as many subscribers as possible. Getting people to sign up for our list is essential, but not if they are the wrong type of people. When we talk about building an email list, we focus on the numbers of subscribers we have more than the quality of those subscribers.

On the other hand, when we phrase our email list as something we are providing, we automatically put our subscribers first, providing them with excellent content that makes their lives better. The providing mindset also forces us as marketers and creators to become more interesting people to have something interesting to share with our subscribers.

Viewing our email list as something we provide puts the focus on connecting with our subscribers. We discussed the same concept earlier in this book when we talked about the five social media marketing myths.

How do you get people to sign up for the list you are *providing*?

The key to getting people to consider joining your list is to give them something they want. How do you know what they want? You talk to them on social media. You engage with them, comment on their posts, DMing them, answering their questions, and consistently scanning your market for new insights. If you do that, you will develop a nose for knowing what your target audience cares for, allowing you to produce a so-called "lead magnet" you can give them in exchange for their email address. If your lead magnet is good, which means it contains better stuff than people can find for free on Wikipedia, and you also *overdeliver* on their expectations, you are on your way to success.

What to send your subscribers, and how often to send it

If it's challenging to get people to join your list, the actual email marketing game begins after they have signed up. When people first sign up, they will typically get your lead magnet and a few pre-written emails (often called a welcome sequence) delivered in the next 1-2 weeks so they can get to know you and your world better. If they like what they get, they will stay on your list, and if they don't, they will unsubscribe (which is fine). After they have finished the welcome sequence, it's your job as the creator to keep serving them with excellent content regularly. I have talked about content creating and copywriting earlier in this book, and it's the same strategies that apply here. Listen to what they say, and always ask yourselves *What's in it for them?*

There are no "rules" of how often you should email your list. Sometimes I send two emails per week, and sometimes I send two per month to my lists. How frequently you send emails to your list is your decision, but a minimum is probably once a month after they have gotten to know you. The more important question is: *do you have something interesting to say that will benefit your subscribers?* If the answer to that question is no, you should probably not send anything.

On the other hand, if the answer is *hell yeah!* - go ahead and send those emails asap! What you are trying to accomplish is to create a bond with your subscribers. You want them to know that the emails you send are interesting and packed with value. You want them to open, read and share your message on your behalf.

Approaching your list like that will push you to find exciting articles/ideas and package that in a way that can benefit your subscribers. And in that process, what you are doing is not just marketing; you make people's lives better. When you reach that point, selling your product/service feels like an obligation.

How to sell in email

Think about all the sales emails you have received over the years. Now think about the last time you bought something from an email. Why did you do that? Probably because you trusted that person, they offered you something you wanted, gave you a reason to buy, and induced a little scarcity.

Selling your product/service in email is as simple as putting in front of the right people, giving them a reason to buy and then leaving the decision up to them, as we talked about in the copywriting section of this book.

If you followed the steps I've discussed in this chapter, you would use social media to get quality email subscribers and slowly build relationships with them. They trust you. They know you have exciting things to say, so selling your product/service will feel natural.

Conclusion

Social media is an excellent, powerful tool that can transform your business into a thriving, well-oiled machine if you use it strategically to your advantage. I hope that through this book, I have provided you with information and things that you should avoid doing as well as those that you should do to succeed. Keep in mind that your goal is to provide compelling content, connect with people, and establish a relationship. Instead of hunting for likes, tricking into clicking methods, you want to create these relationships through your ability to provide them with what they need and express it so that each person feels heard and feels an emotional connection.

Start by avoiding the myths and use the tools, skills, and strategies that you have on hand to make your email list grow. Because after all, you may have many people following your page – but unless you own your platform and control if they see your message or not, it might all be for nothing.

Connect with the author

There are plenty of great books out there, so thank you for choosing this one and reading to the end!

I hope I have given you something worth your time, despite not being a native English writer.

What I hate after reading a book is the feeling that it's stuffed with bad and boring content that's easily found for free online. If I gave you that, let me know in the reviews. But, on the other hand, If I gave you what you expected (or more), please tell me that in the reviews!

If you want to connect with me, learn all about Swedish Fika, and get my monthly marketing email Swedish Fika and Marketing Strategies, go to

christianoberg.com/strategies

Regards,
Christian Oberg
christianoberg.com
IG: @inkomstmedbocker

More Books by Chris Oberg

Many people want to make money online but don't know where to start or how to do it.

One way to make money online is by selling ghostwritten books on Amazon, and this book teaches you exactly how.

With the help of this book, you will learn how to produce, publish and market books on Amazon that can generate income for you every month for a long time to come. It contains my experiences of how I have gone about making over $100,000 in royalties from the books I've published on Amazon.

After reading the book, you will have learned:

- How do you write/produce a book you know Amazon customers want to buy.
- How to publish your book in the right way so Amazon customers can find and buy it.
- How authentic marketing can get Amazon to start selling your book for you.
- Strategies to succeed with paid advertising.
- How to scale up book sales and earn passive income.
- And much more!

Are you ready to see the possibilities on Amazon with entirely new eyes? **Read E-Royalties.**

© Copyright 2022 - All rights reserved.

The content contained within this book may not be reproduced, duplicated, or transmitted without direct written permission from the author or the publisher.

Under no circumstances will any blame or legal responsibility be held against the publisher, or author, for any damages, reparation, or monetary loss due to the information contained within this book, either directly or indirectly.

CPSIA information can be obtained
at www.ICGtesting.com
Printed in the USA
BVHW042257090223
658260BV00005B/85

9 789198 681413